thank you

r ayuyang, e baek, a baumgold, a bobco, o broudy, j brown,
e braun, s burnham, m burrows, d cameron, b carman, m chesse,
s cline, p&d x cohen, j covey, a debotton, c dekay, a feuchtenberger,
t fujimaru, n gaiman, t garritty, c giglio, b kersey, l&w gladding,
m goldberg, n&n gordon, m goudeau, m groening, j gunn,
n hathaway, k hauser, k holmes, p jillette, c krol, h letham, j marion,
m matsumiya, s matthews, jc menu, m meyer, d nadel,
k&c nevill-manning, r olsen, l park, l pien, r pike, l pine,
p provenza, g reynolds, j richardson, c sayo, t schantz, e schmitt,
r sohn, t spurgeon, g sorrels, g, d&s stockdale, c summers,
s tejaratchi, s teplin, j tinder, b warnock, d williams, j woodring,
j veeder

h day
renée french

picturebox
po box 24744
brooklyn ny 11202
www.pictureboxinc.com

published by picturebox. all material
herein copyright 2010 renée french.
no part of this publication may be
reproduced without the permission of
the author or publisher. first edition.

isbn 978-0-9820947-0-9. available
through d.a.p./distributed art
publishers.

printed in china

for rob

renée french

picturebox inc., brooklyn

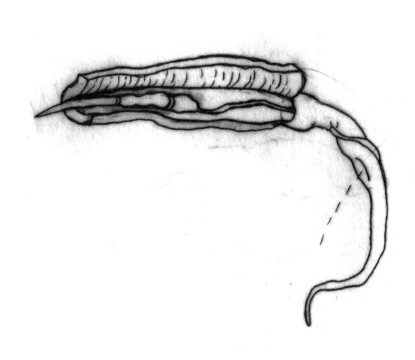

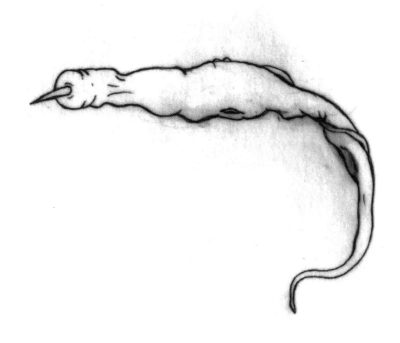

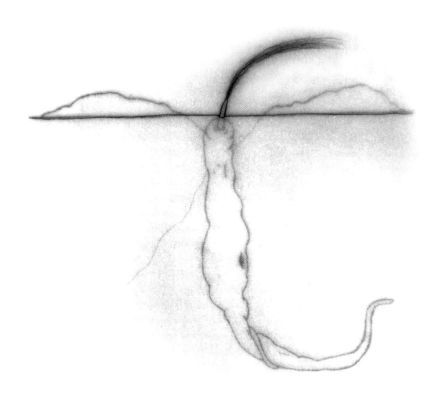

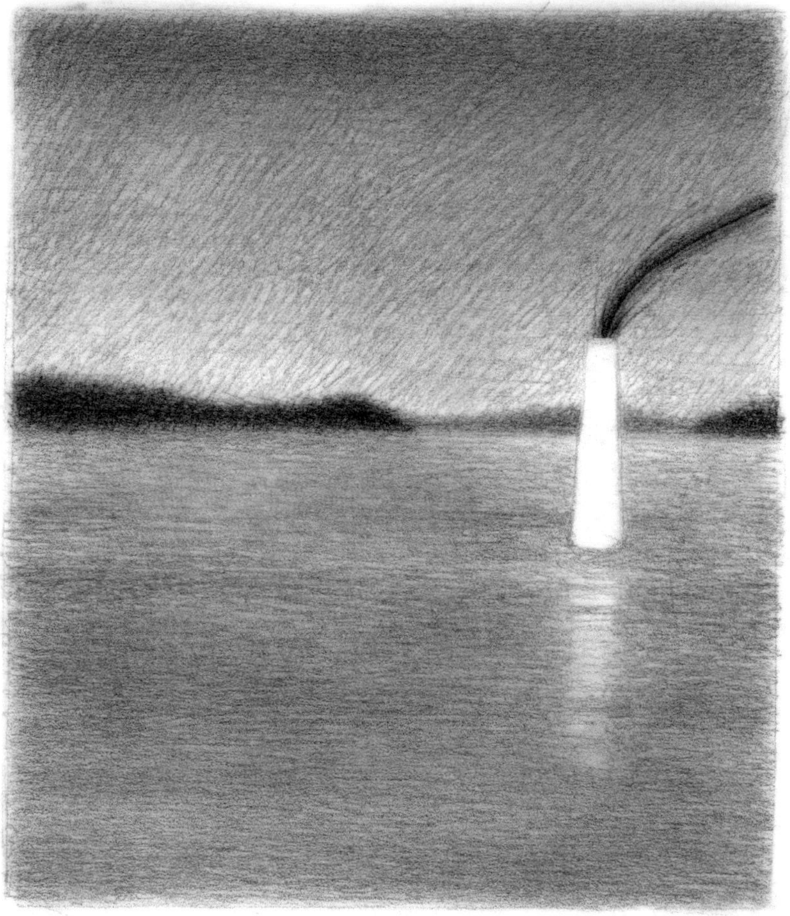

stage I

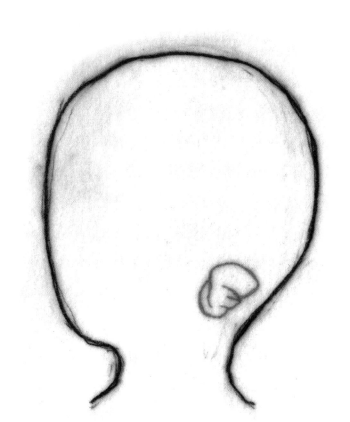

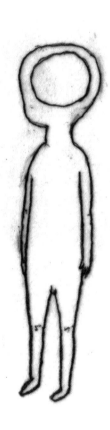

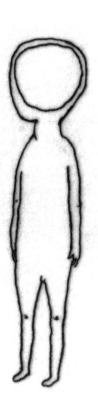

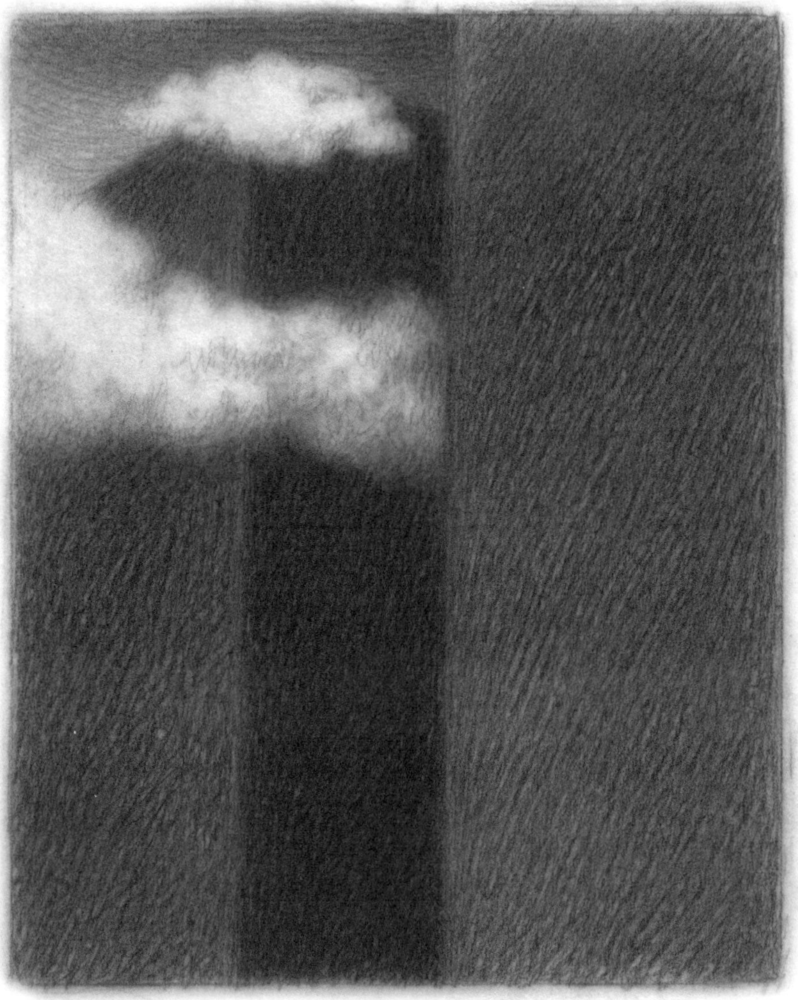

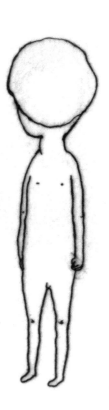

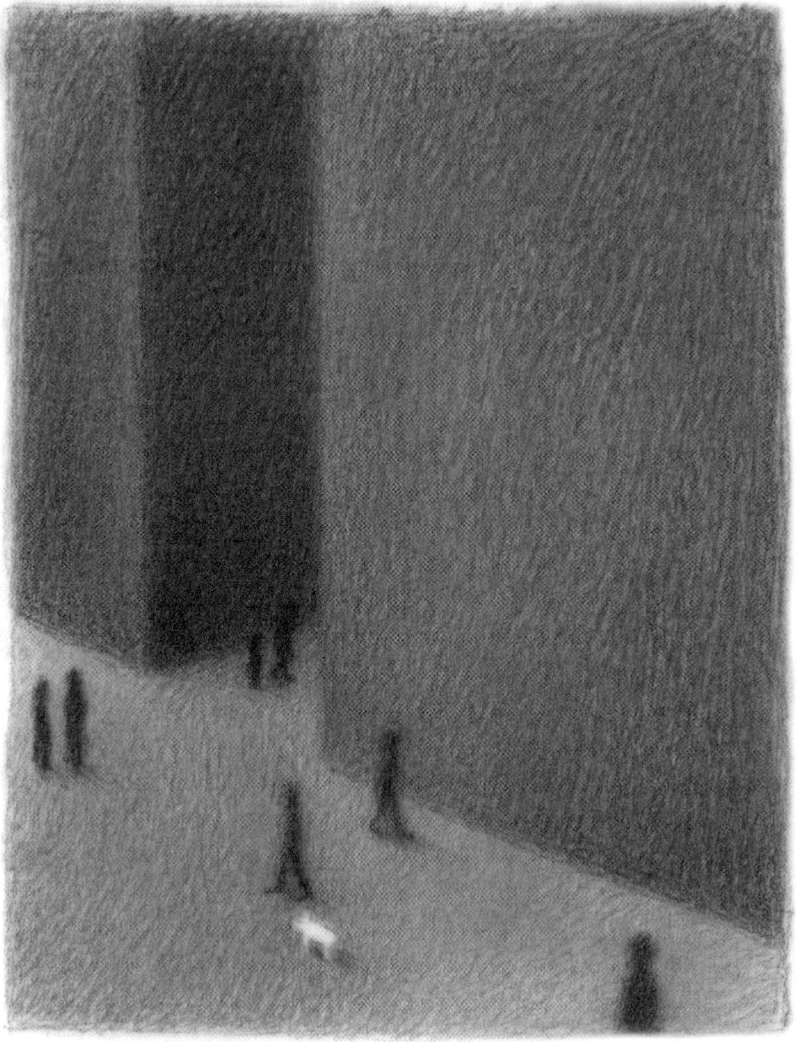

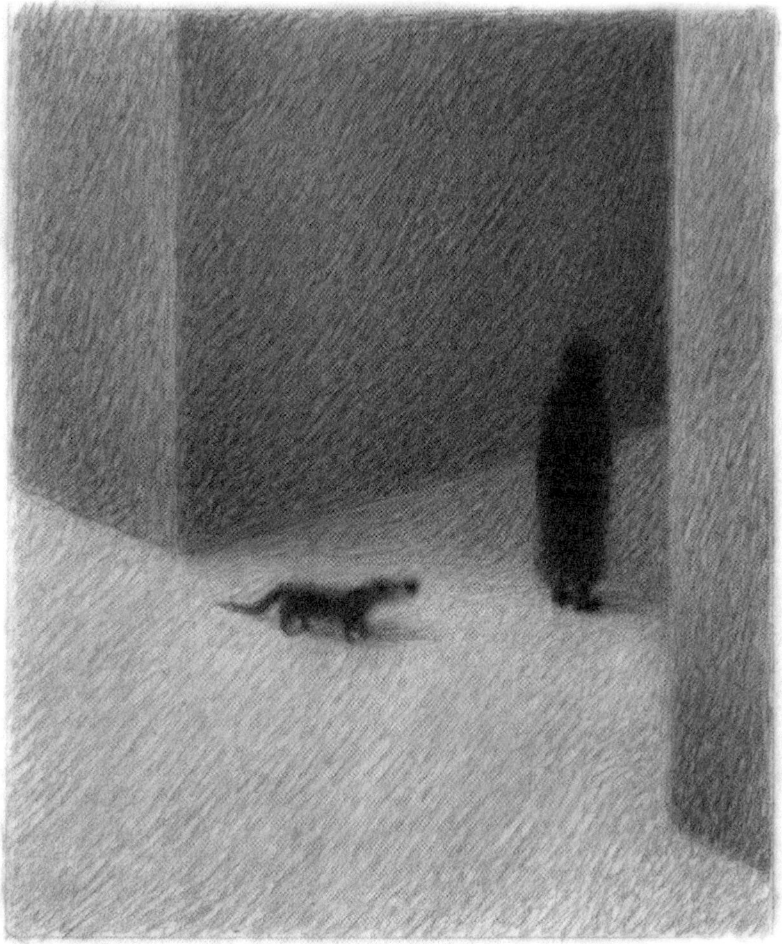

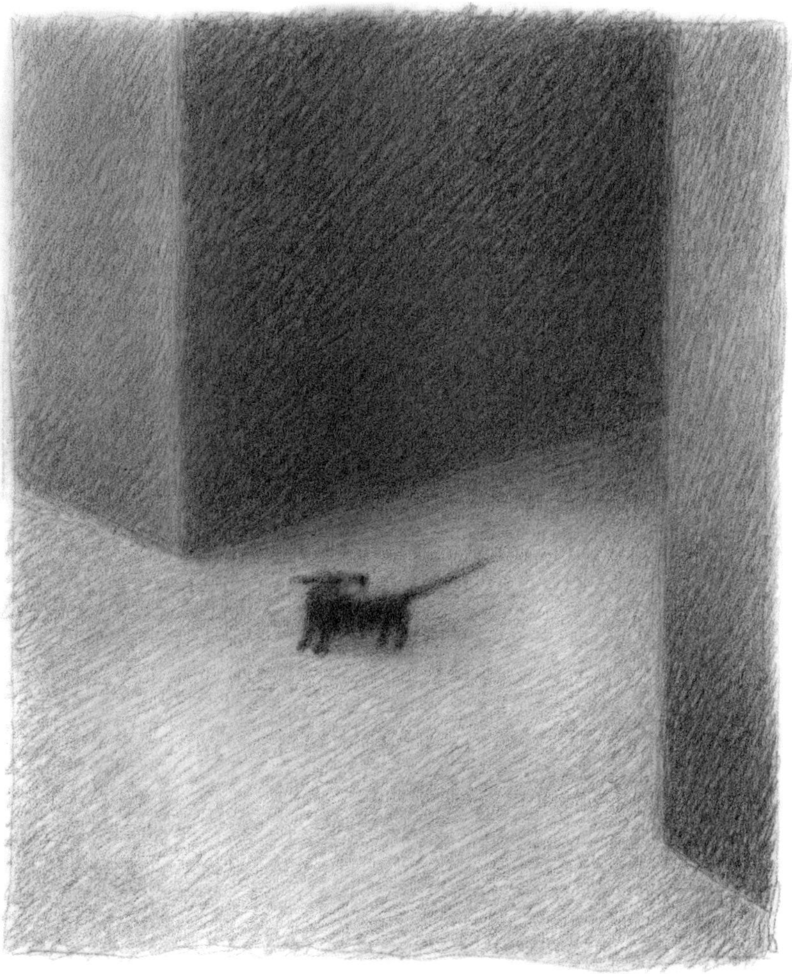

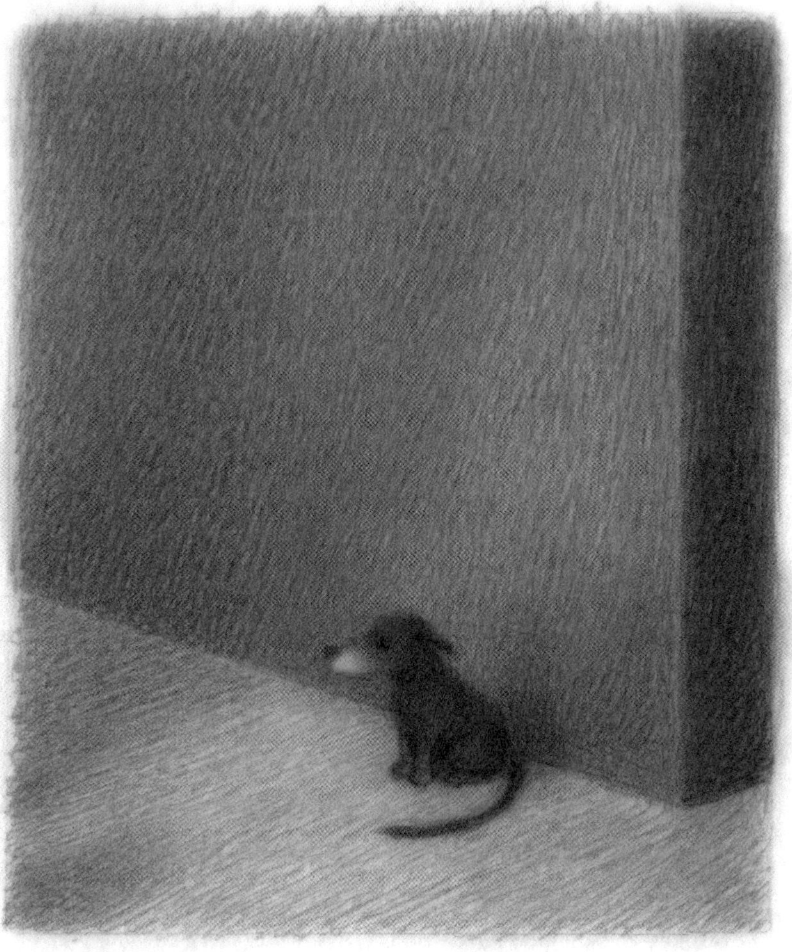

stage 2

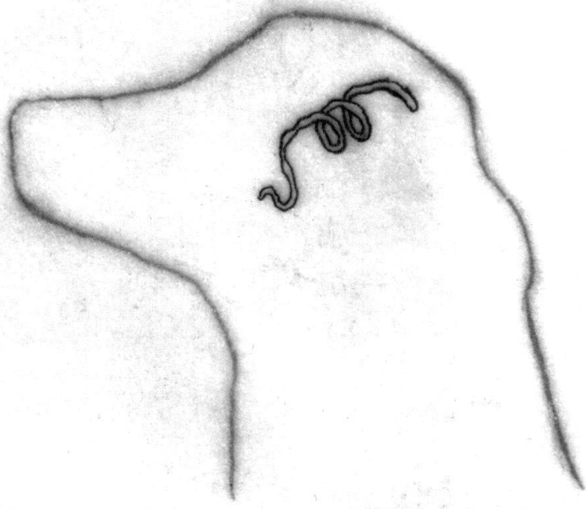

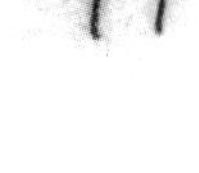

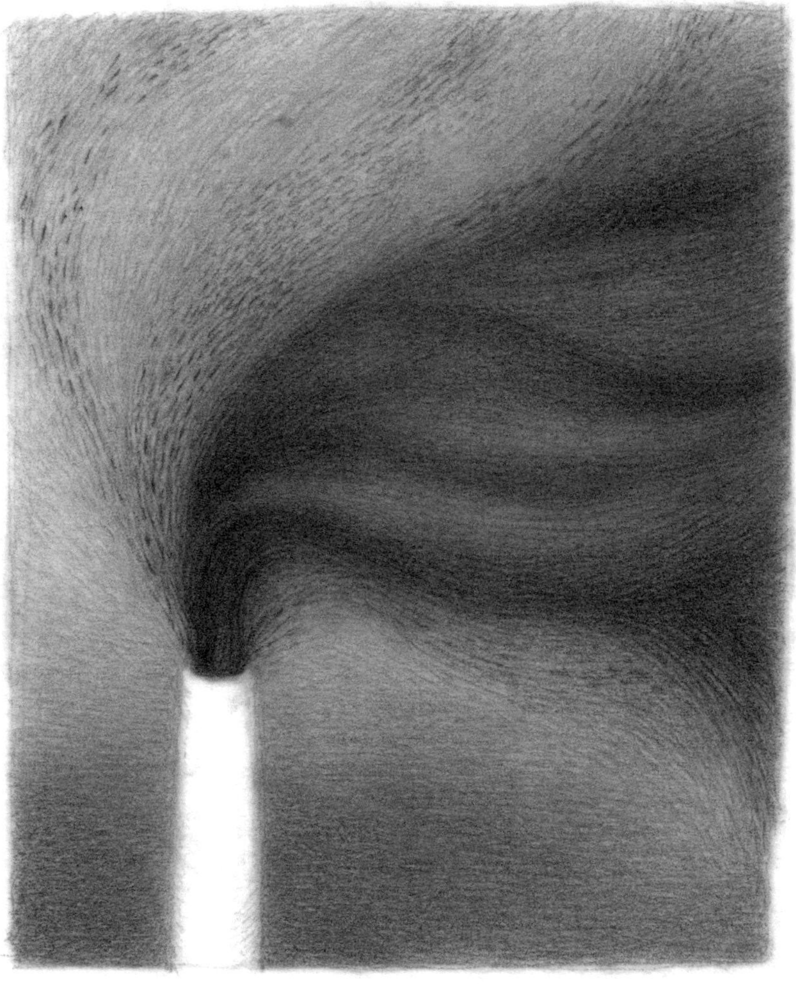

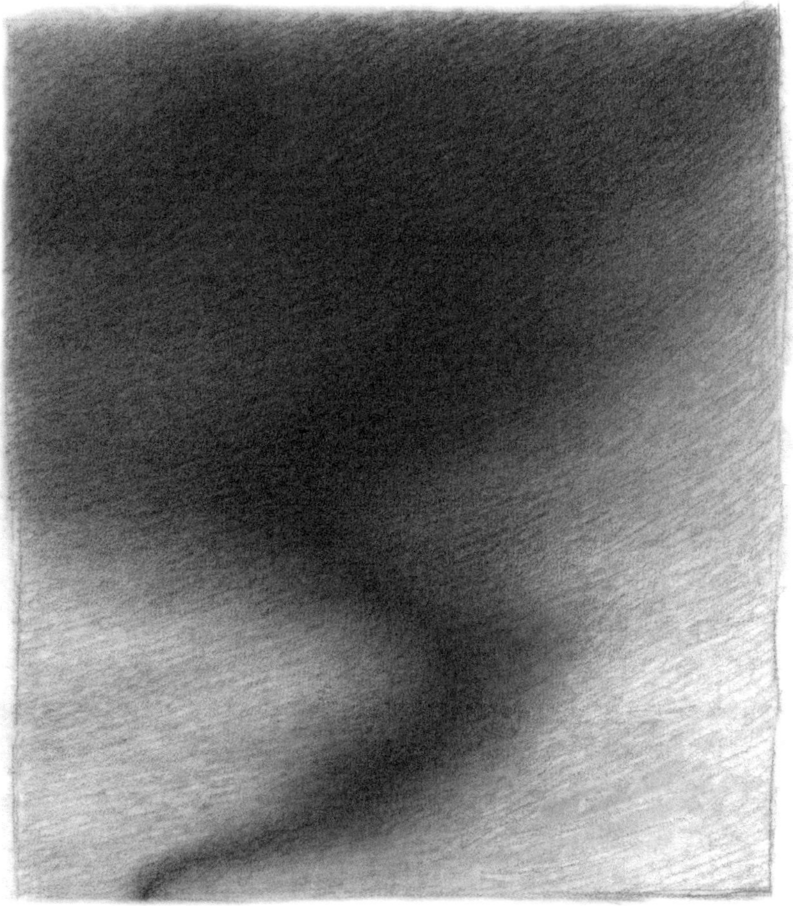

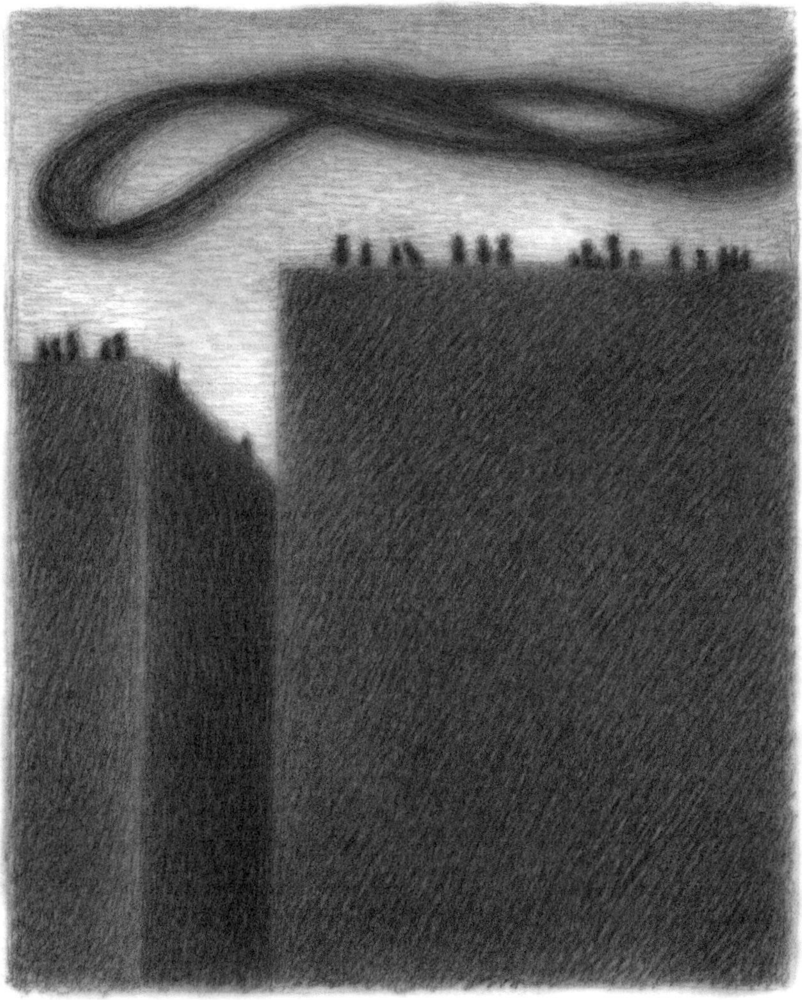

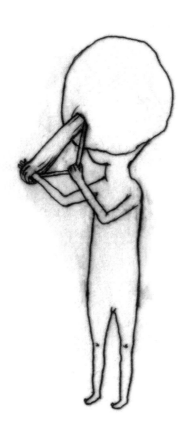

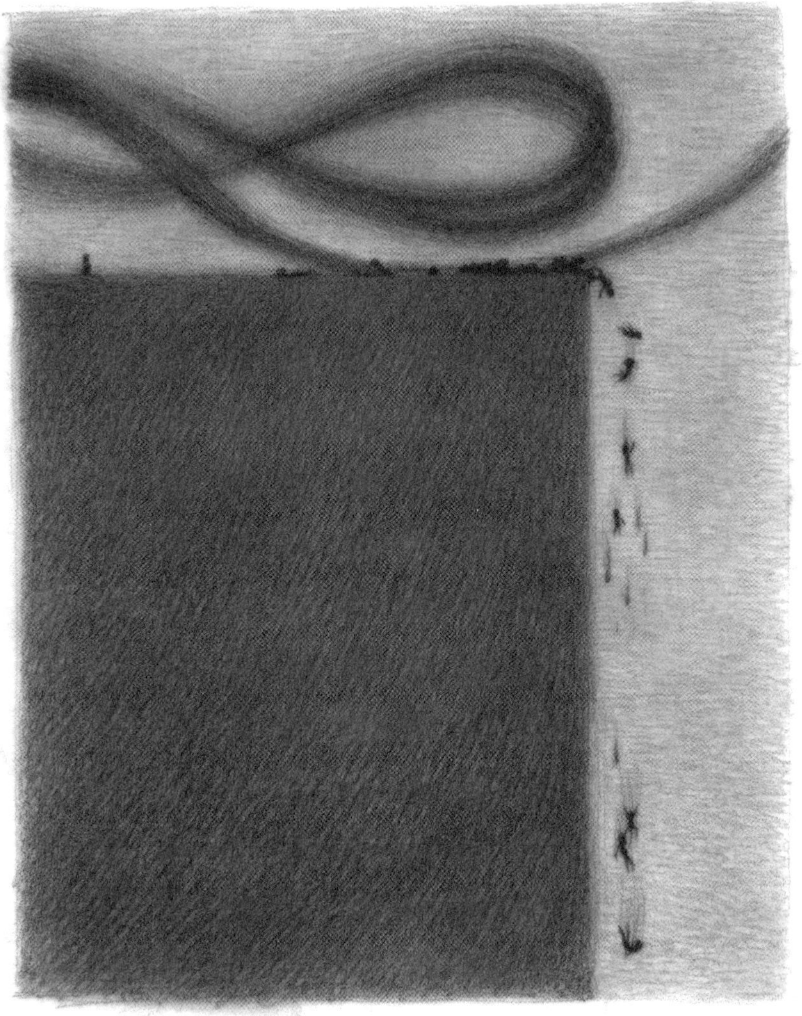

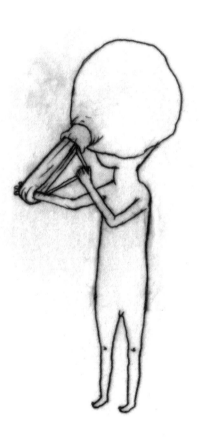

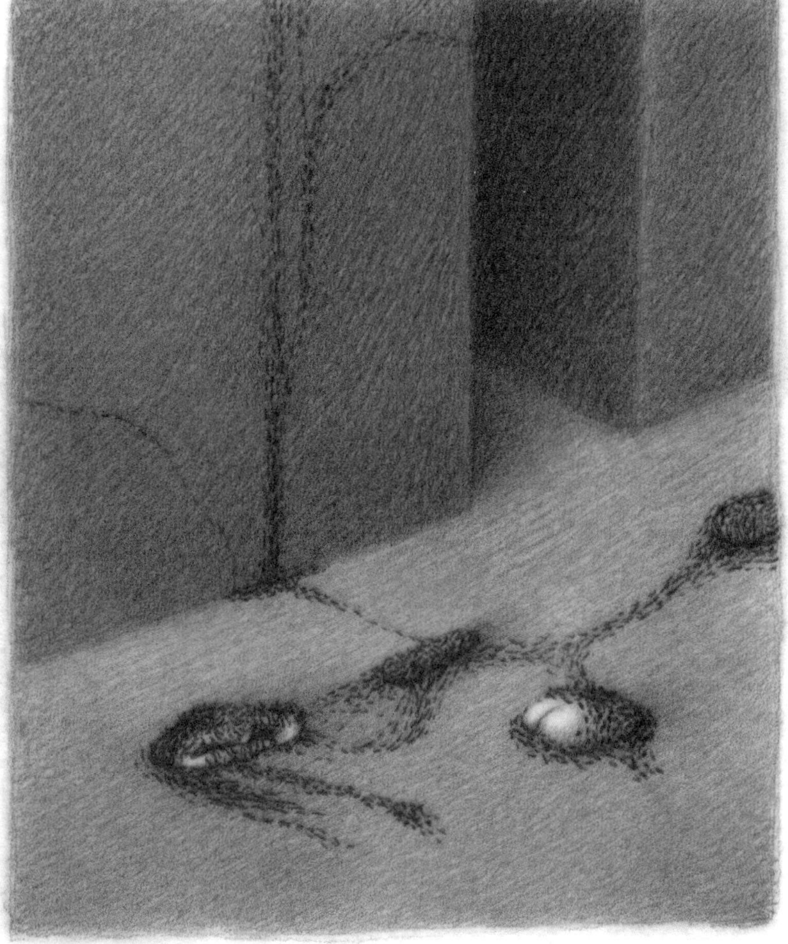

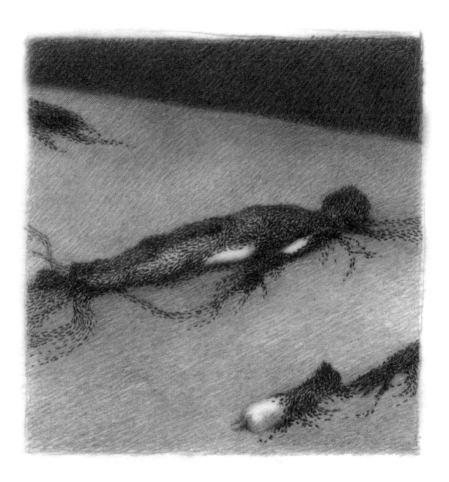

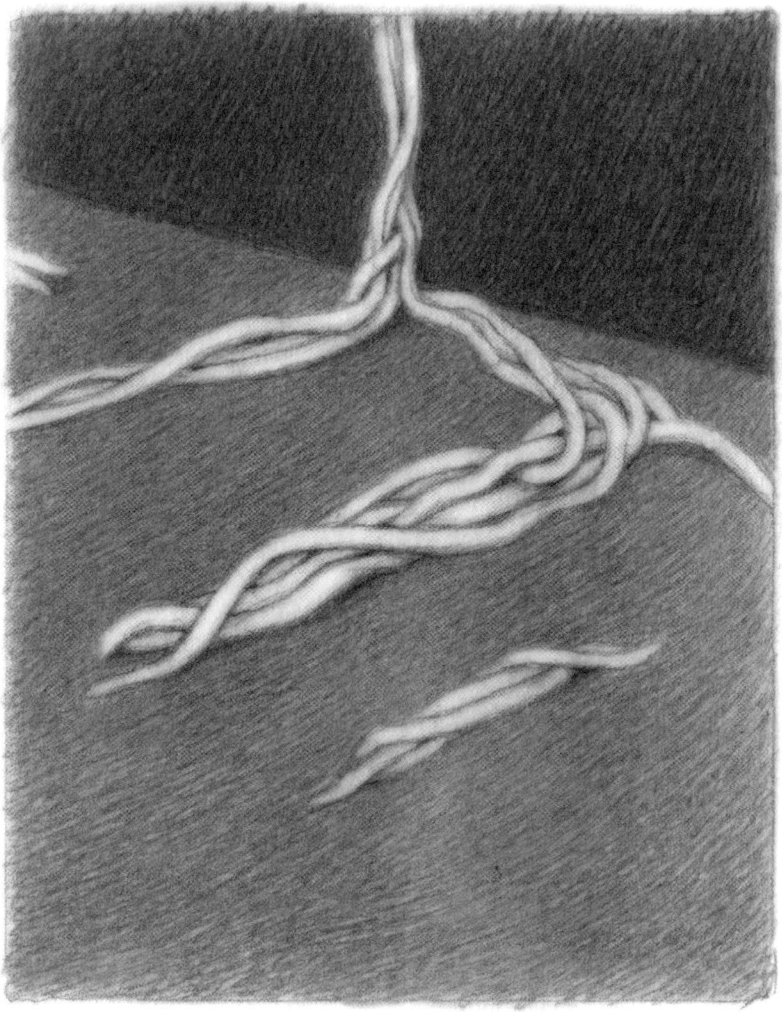

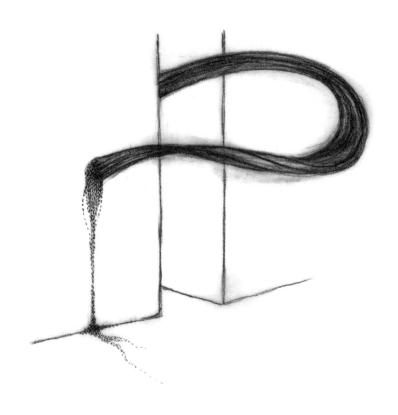

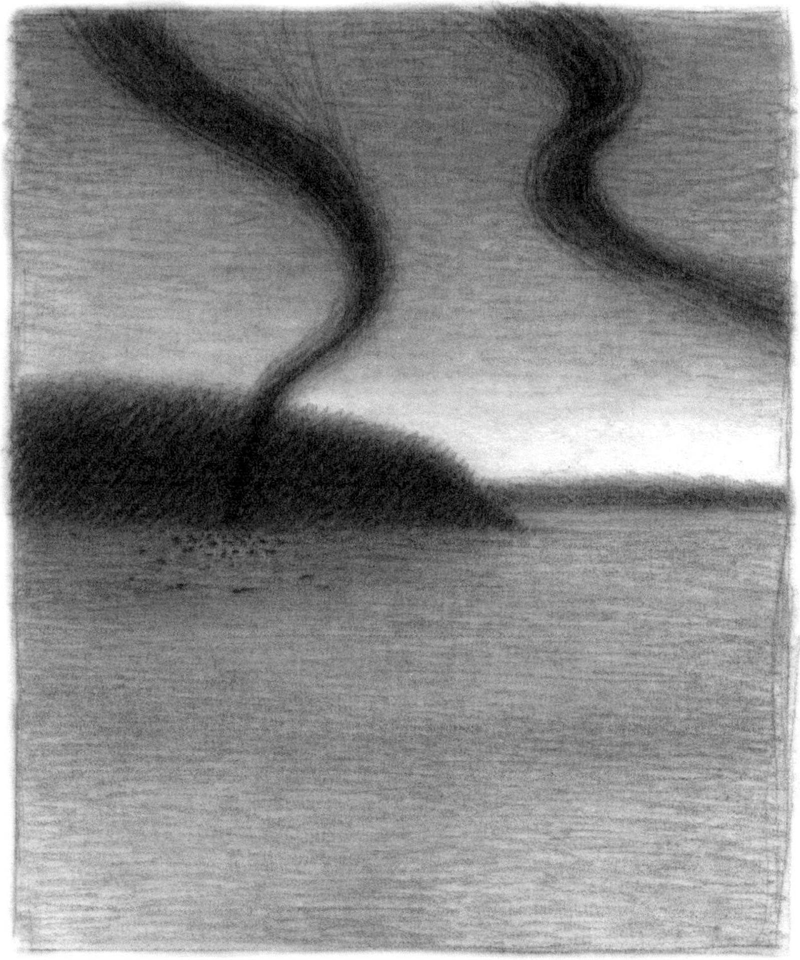

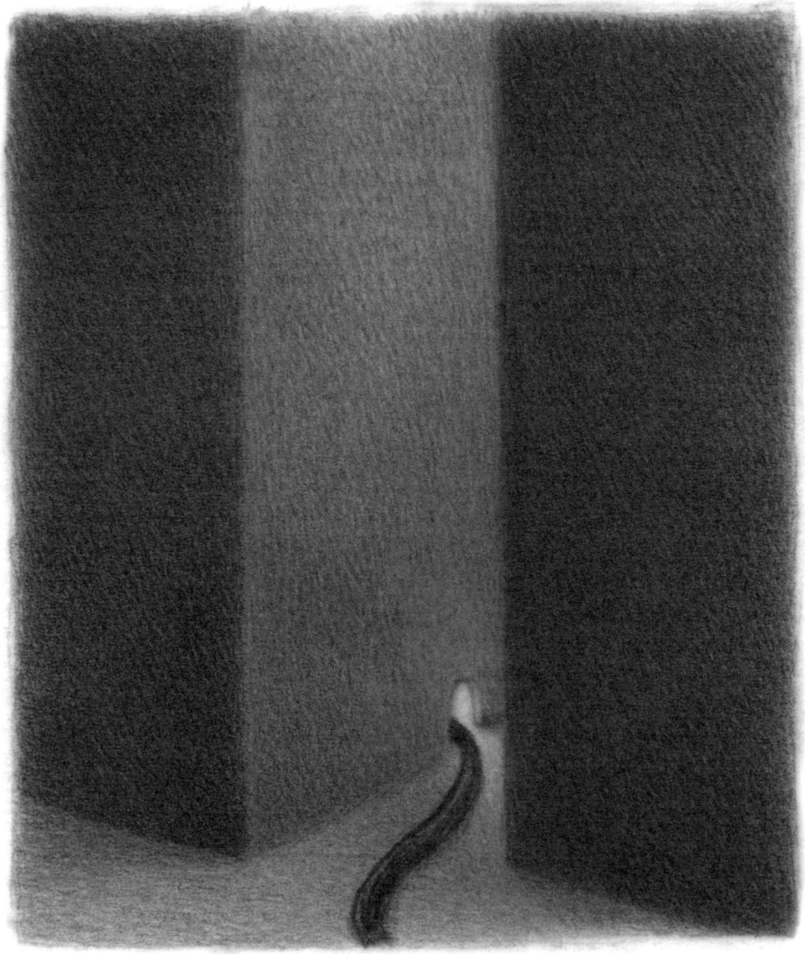

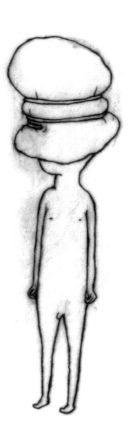

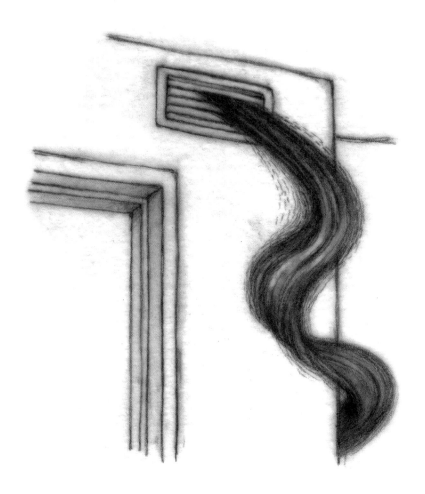

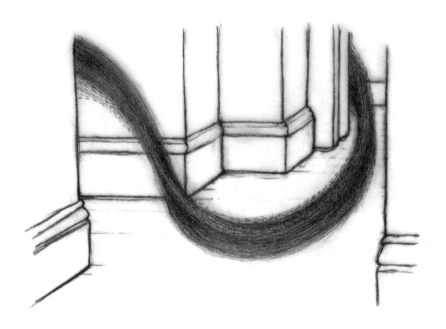

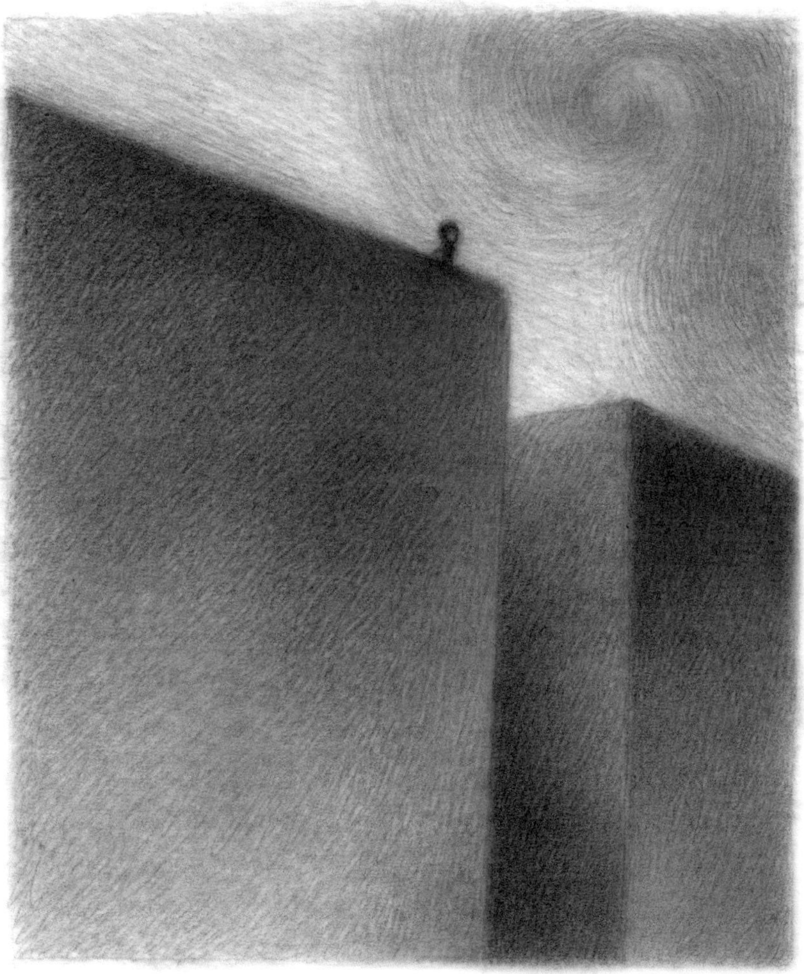

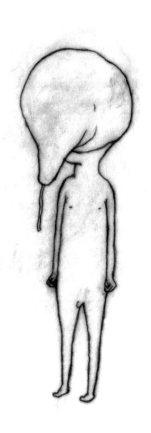

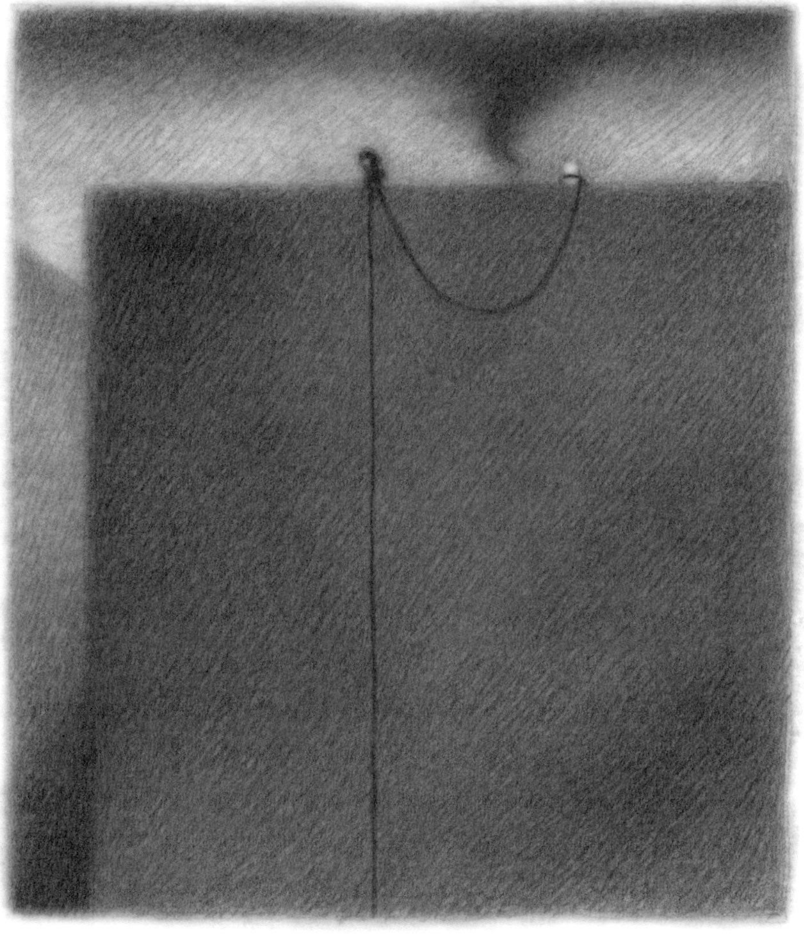

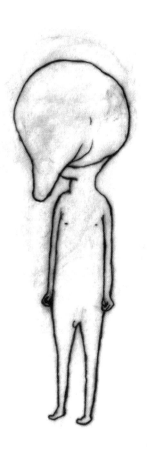

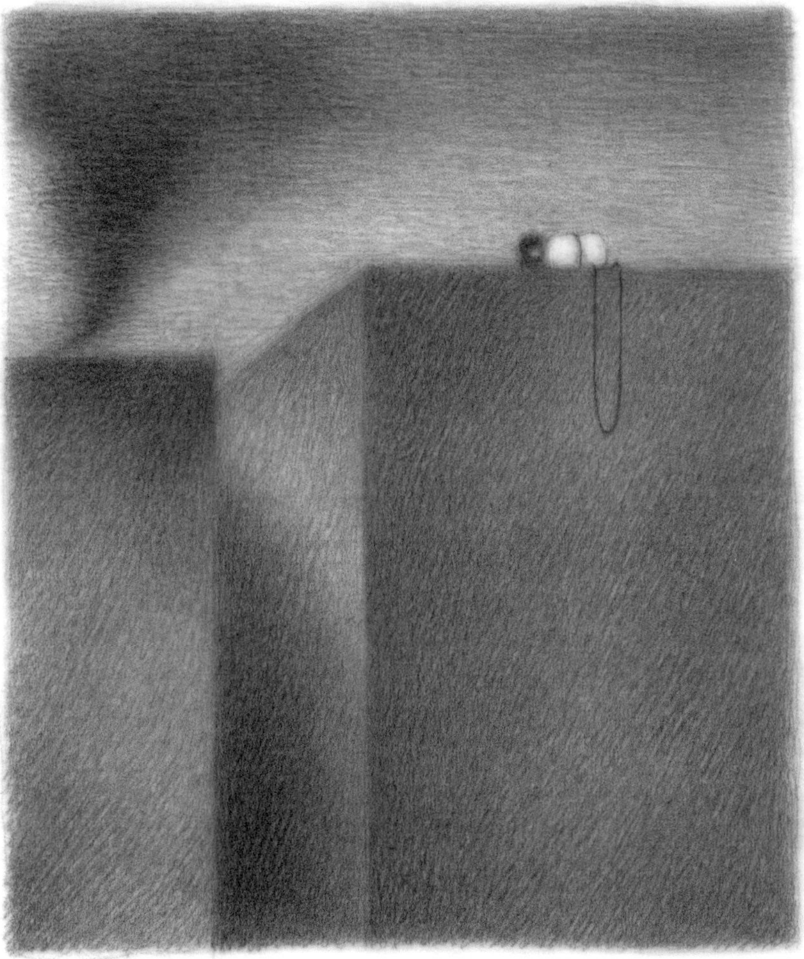

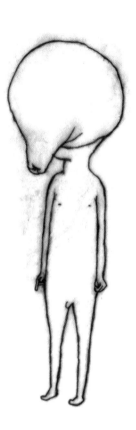

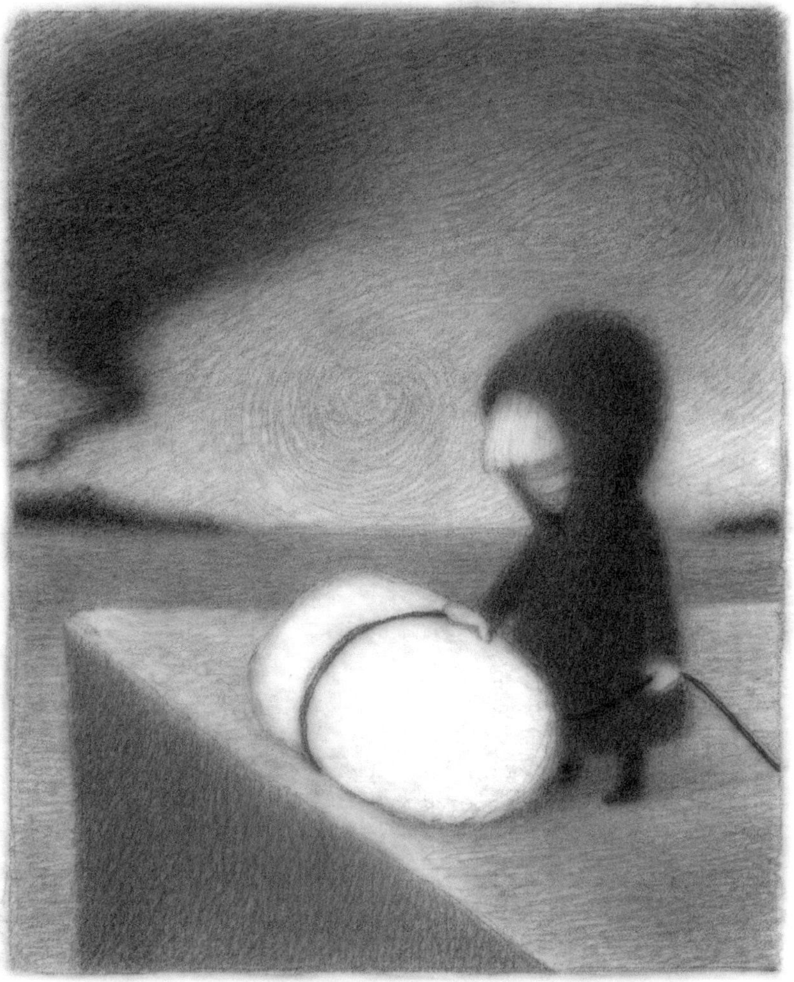

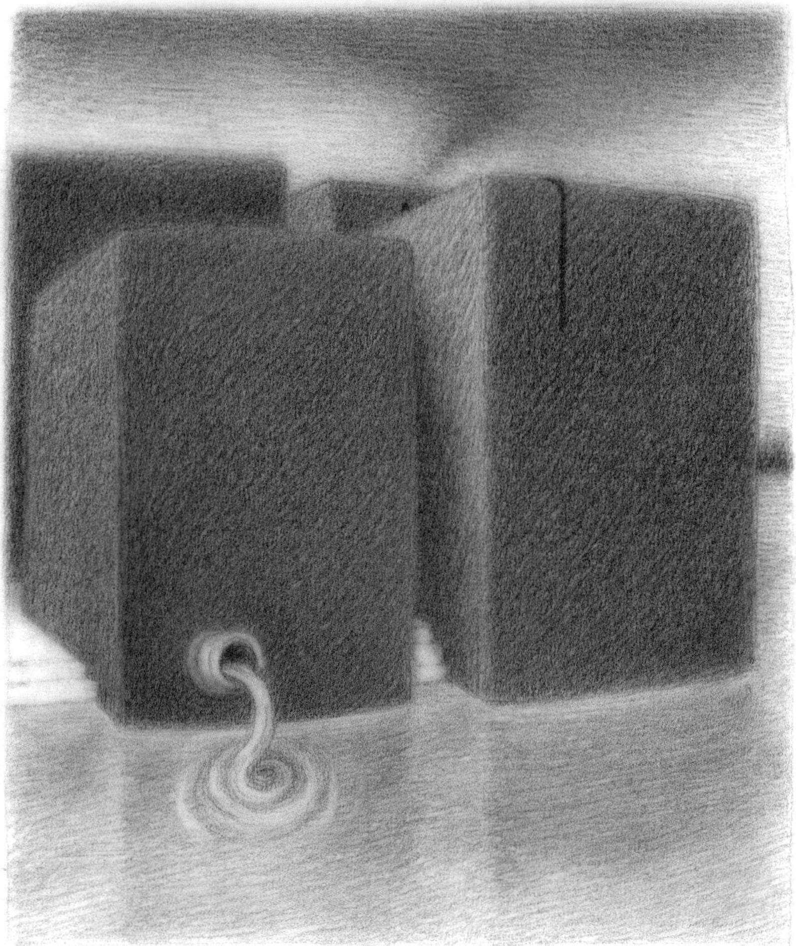

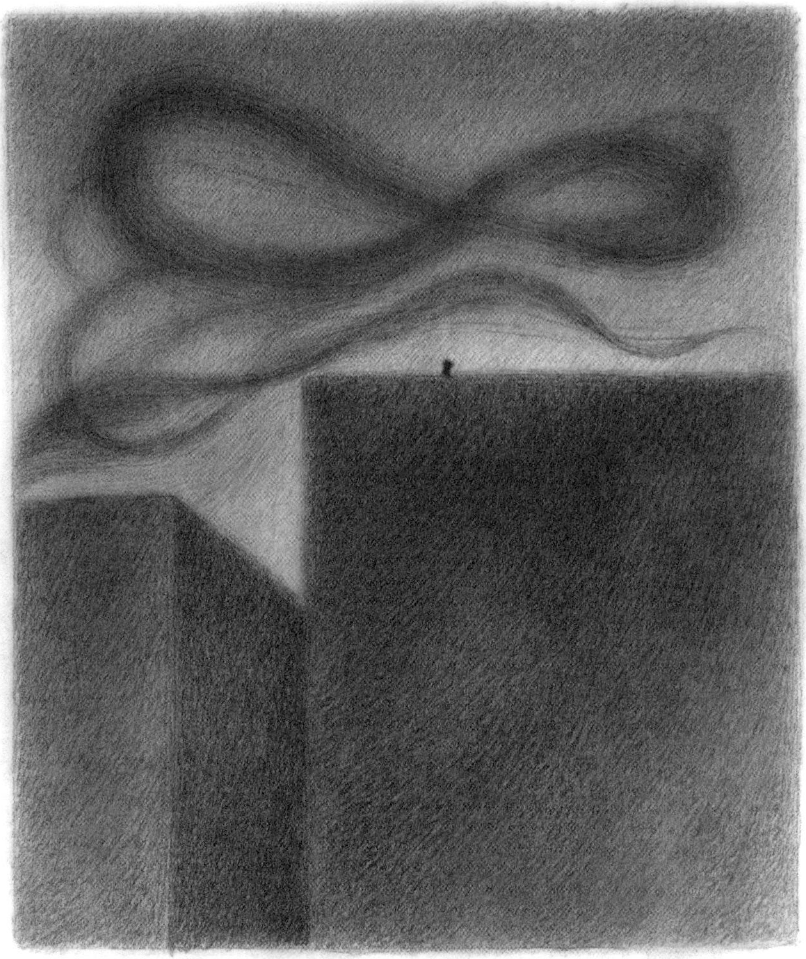

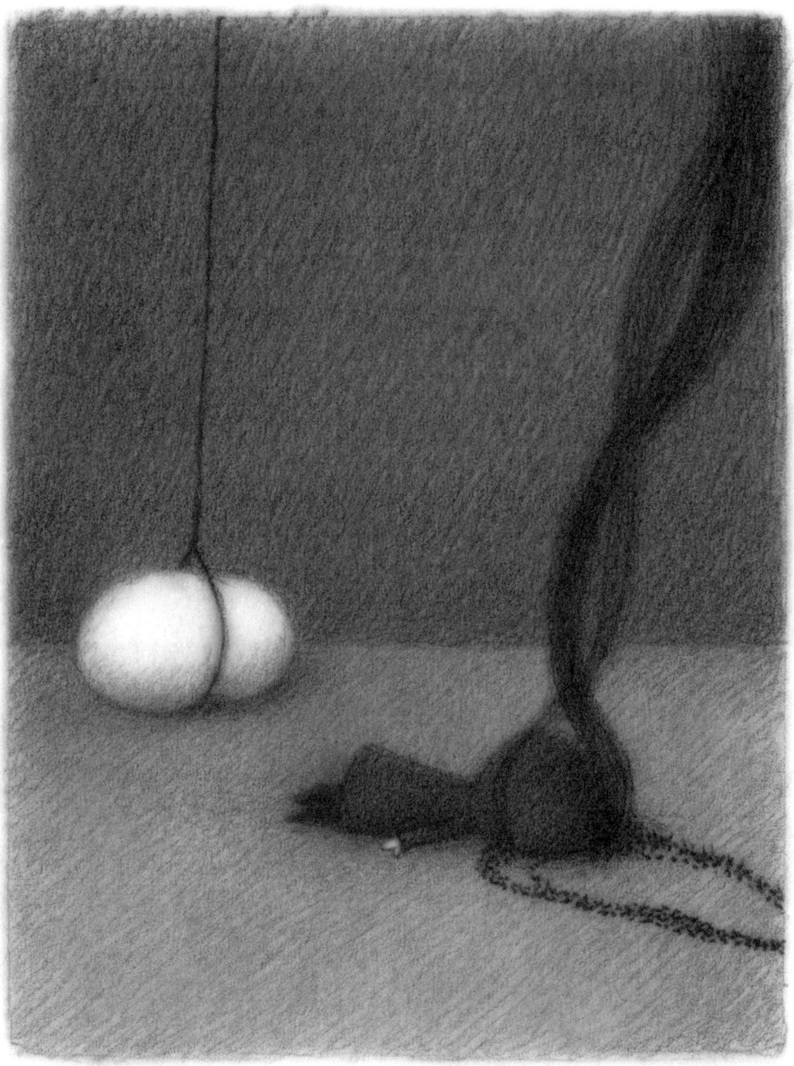

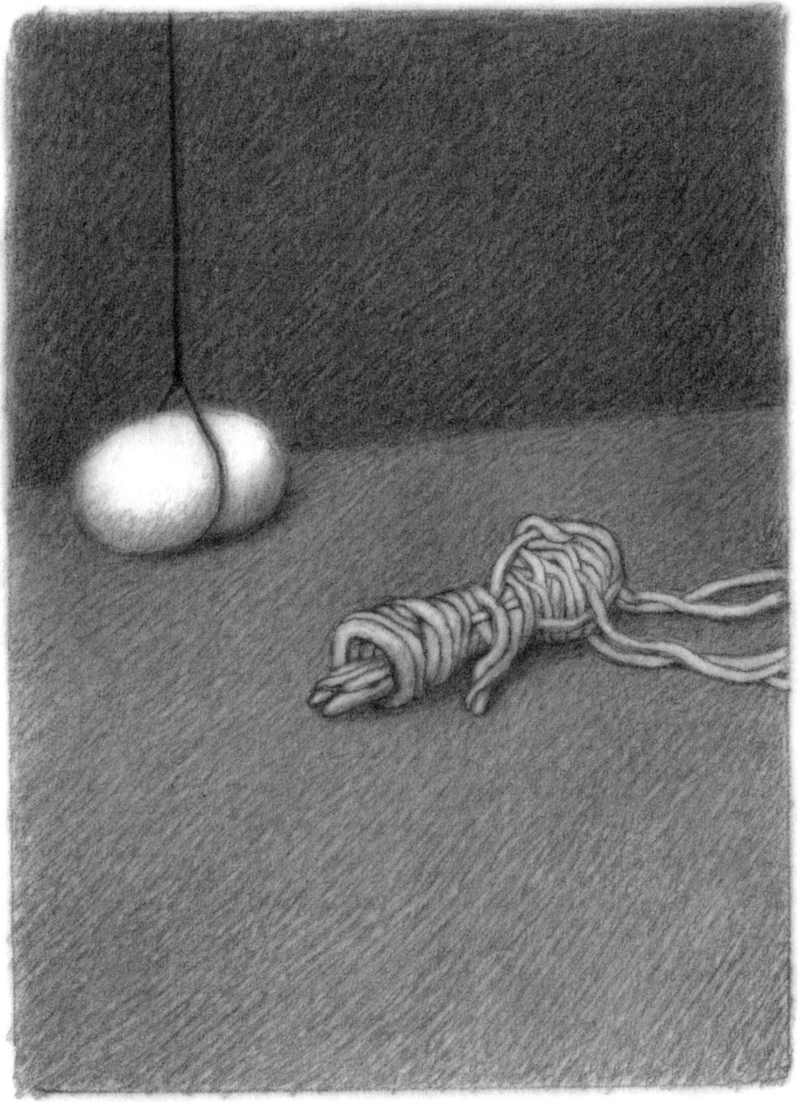

stage 3

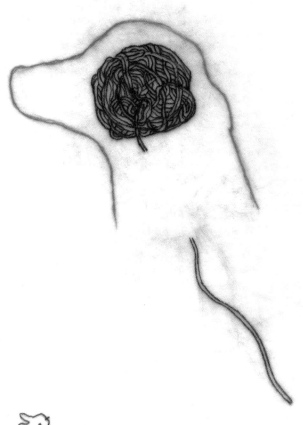

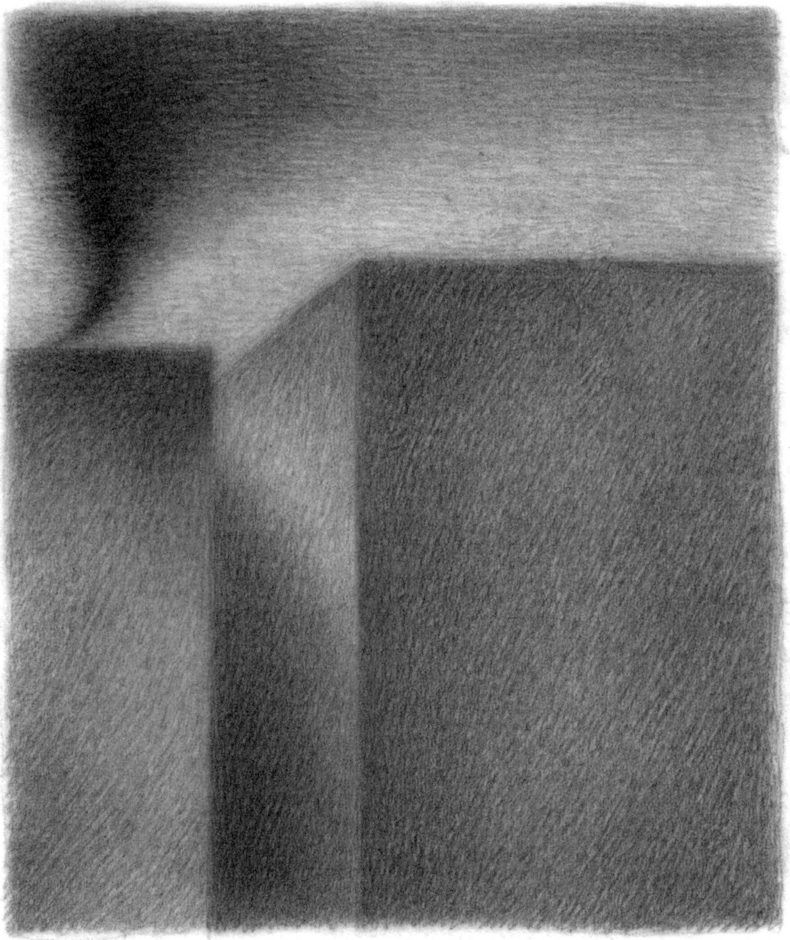

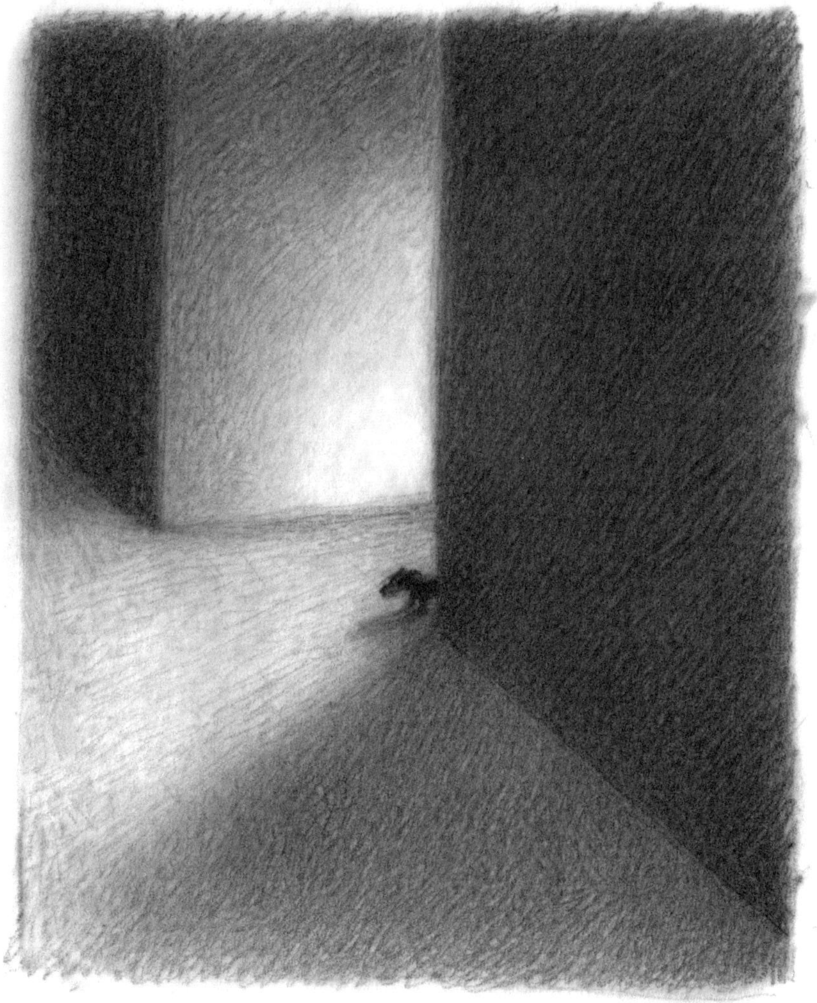

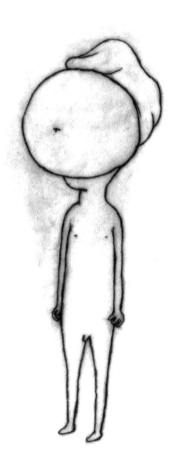

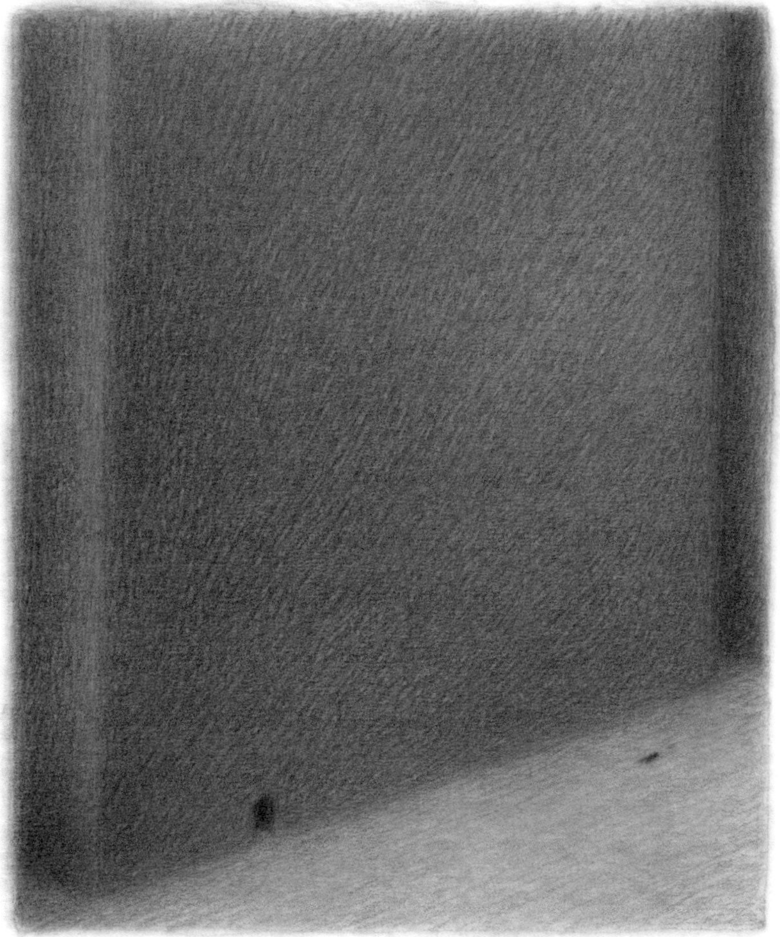

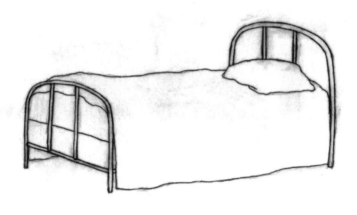

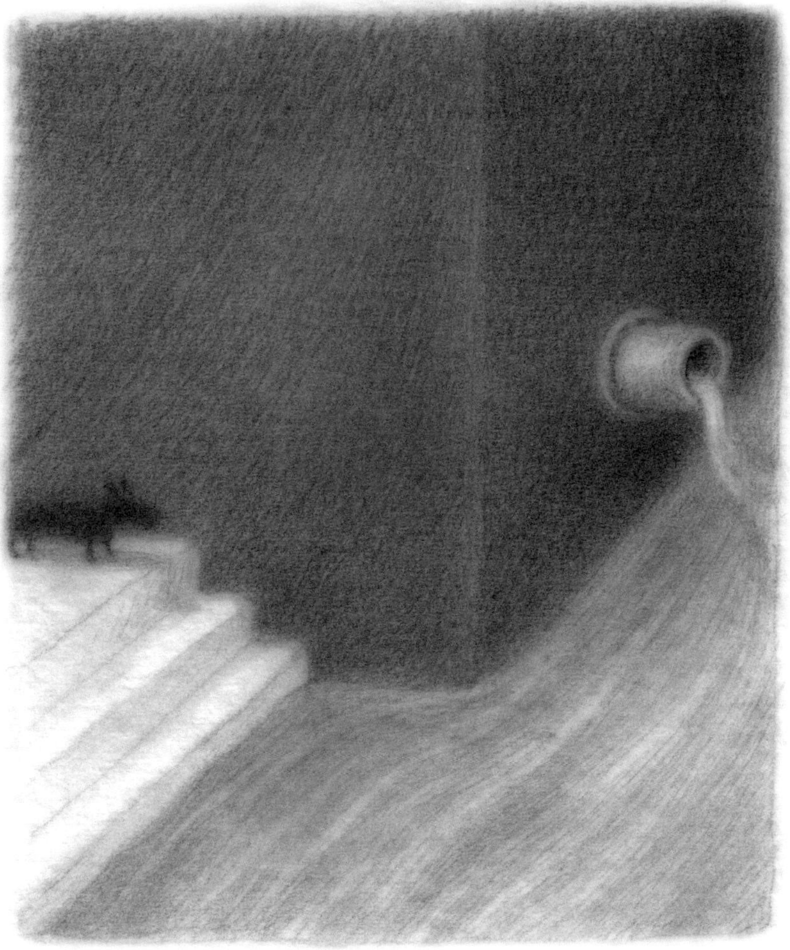

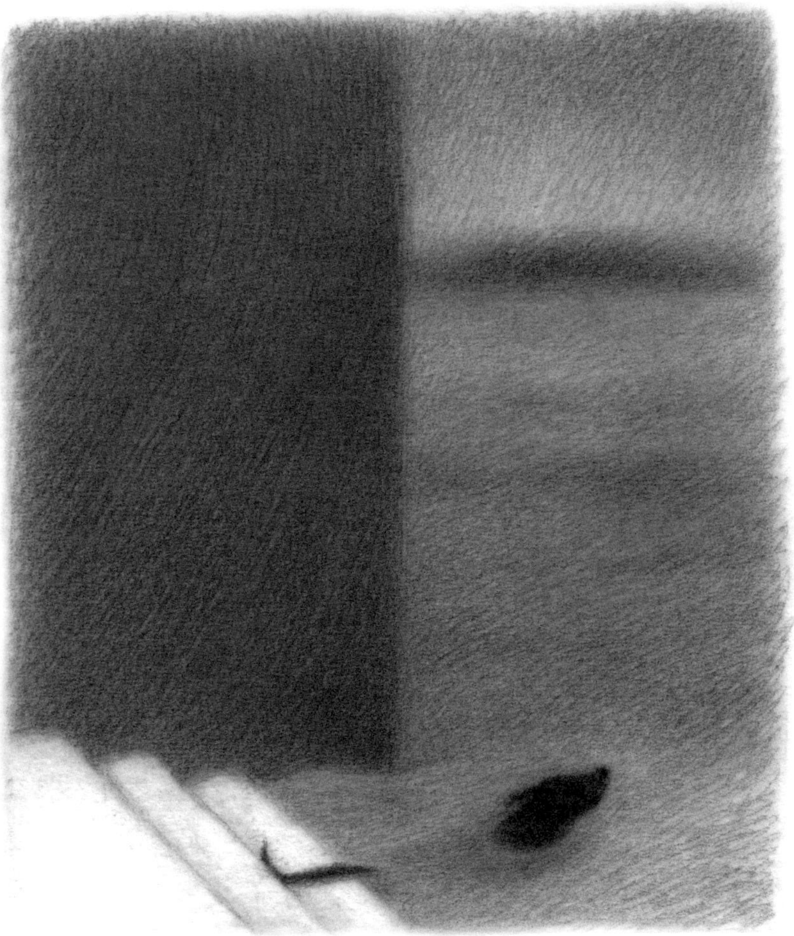

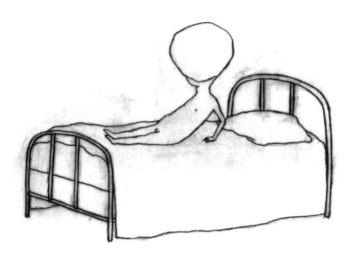

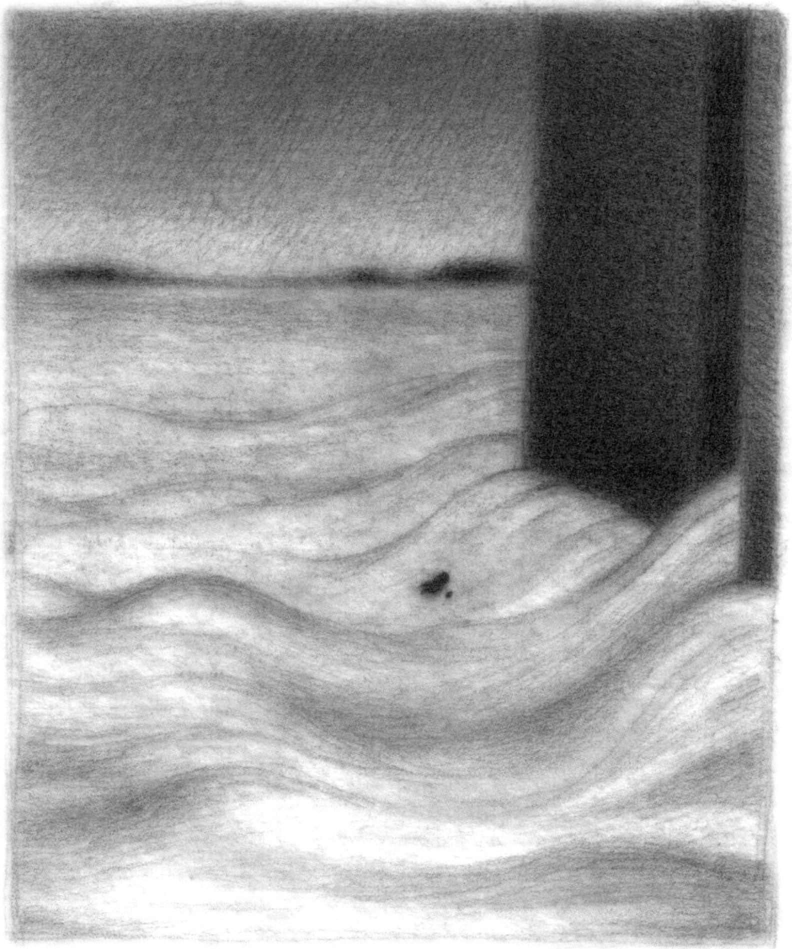

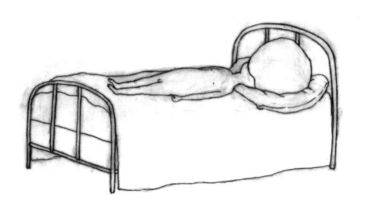

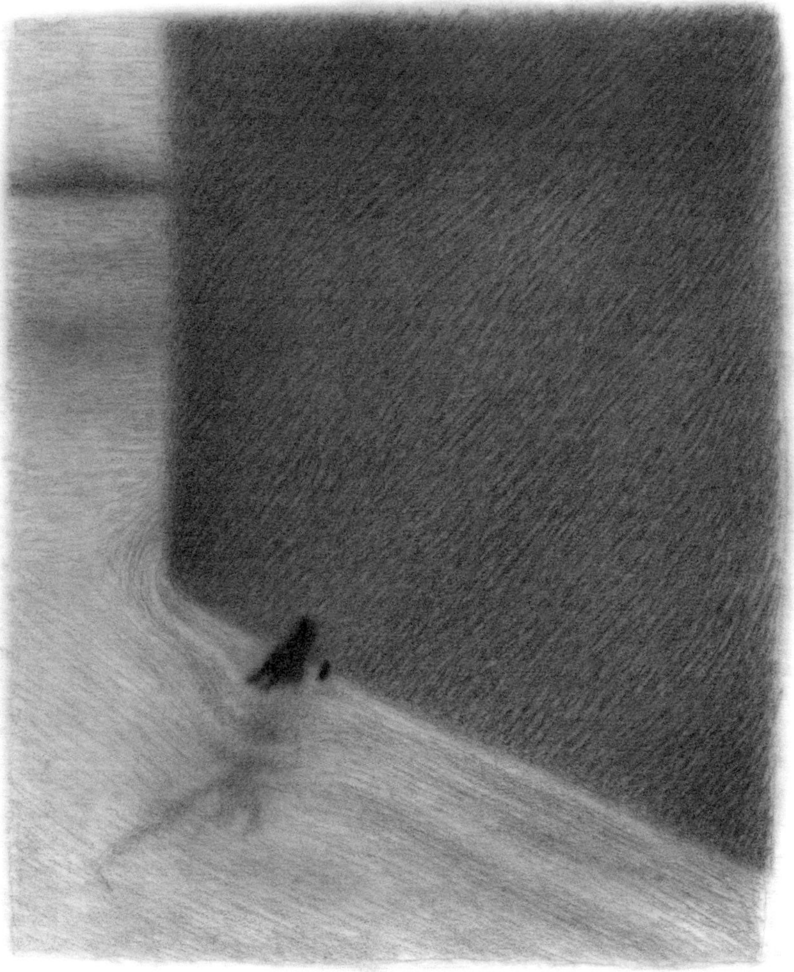

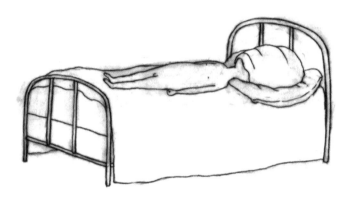

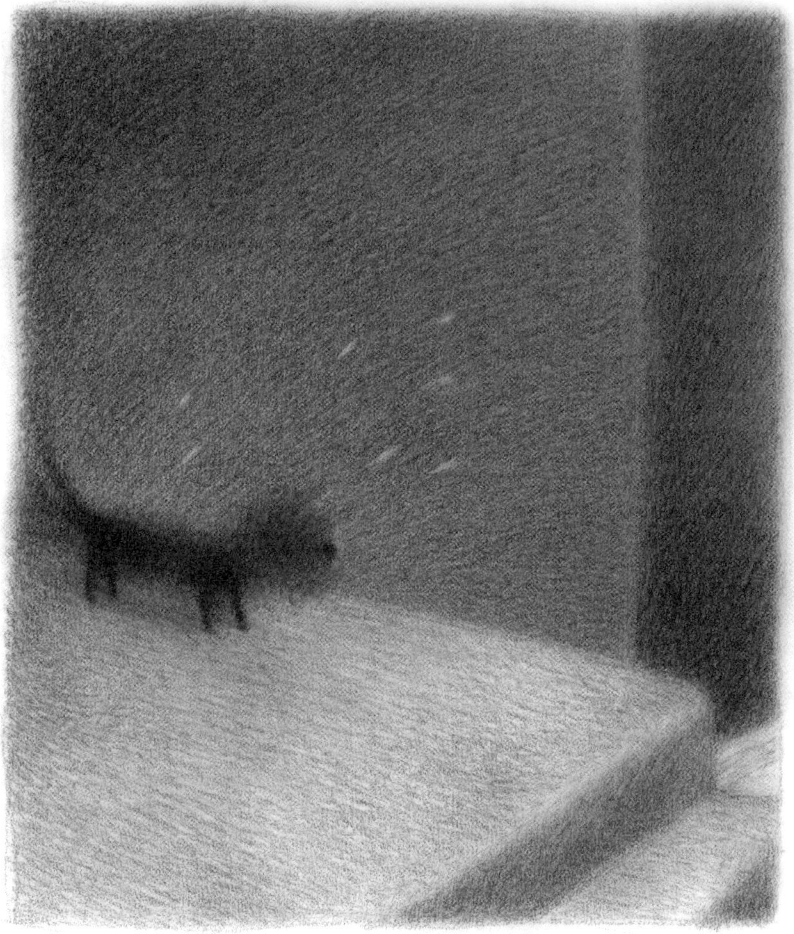

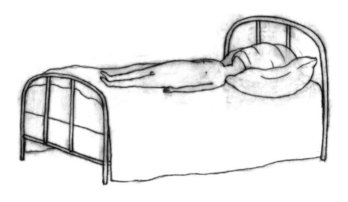

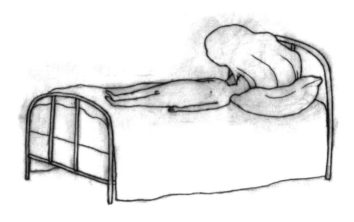

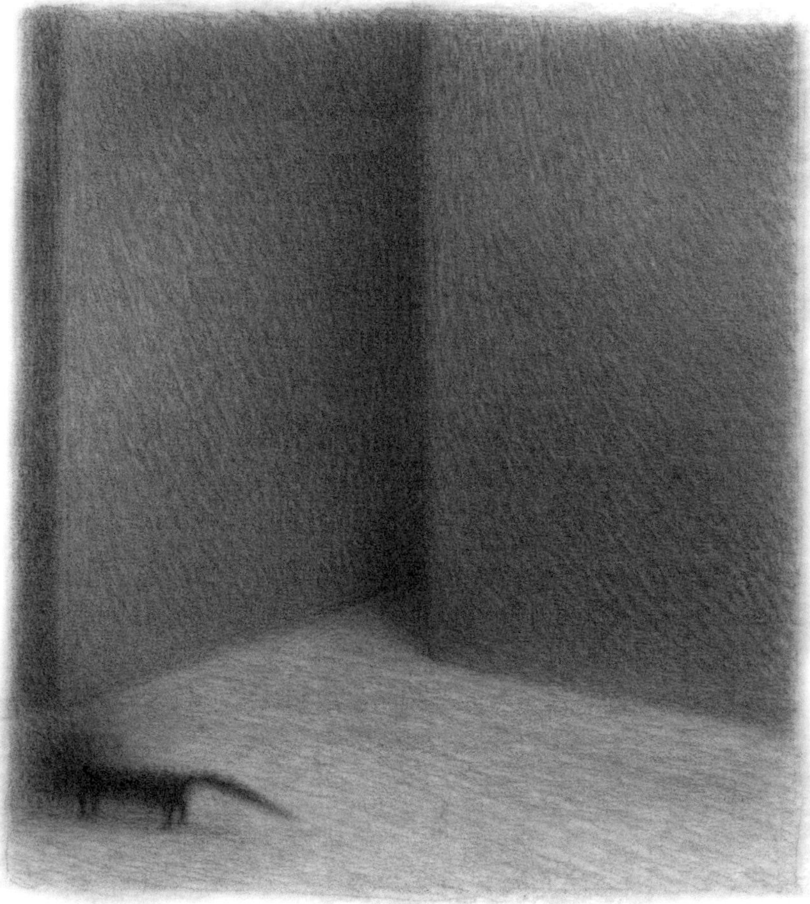

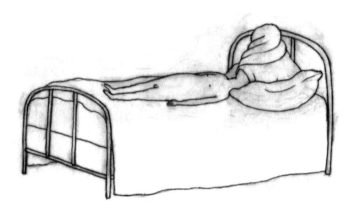

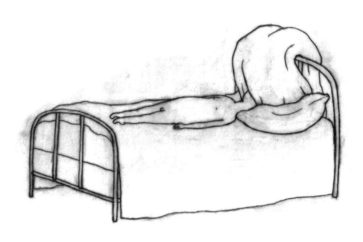

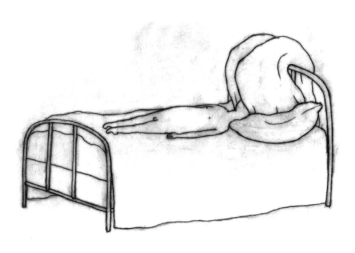

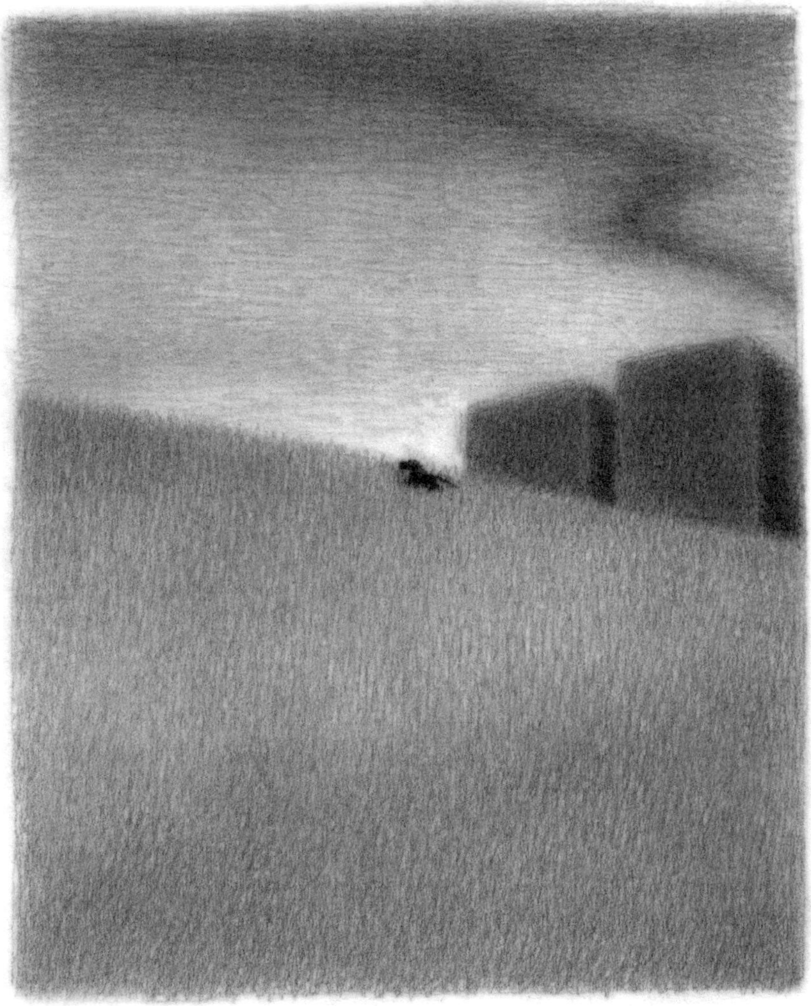

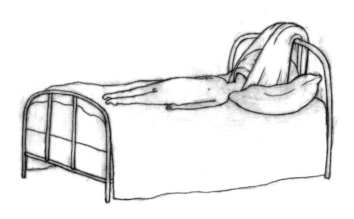

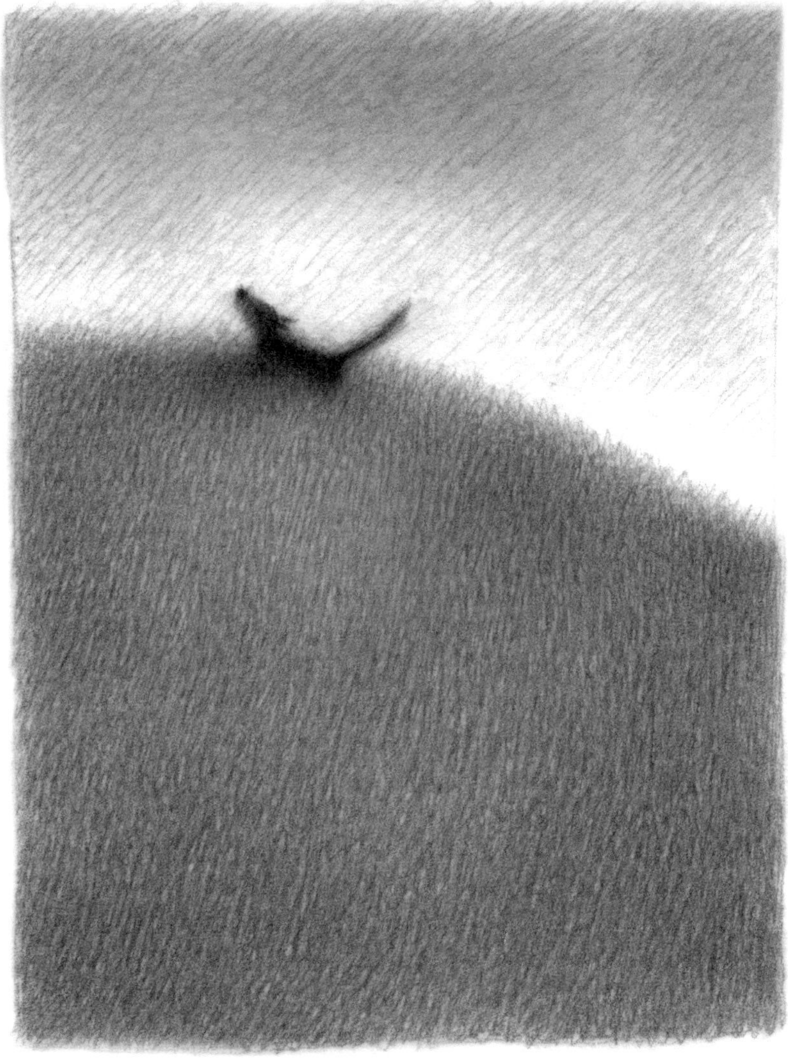

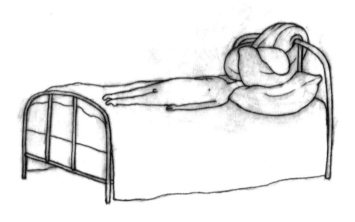

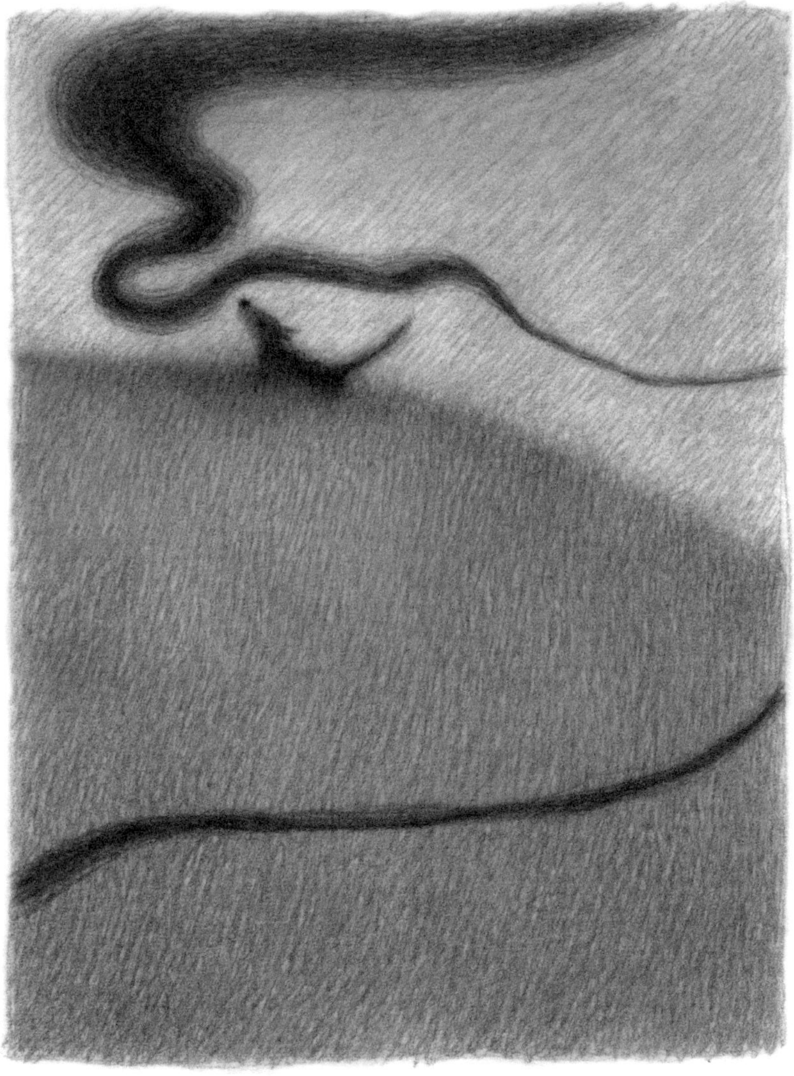

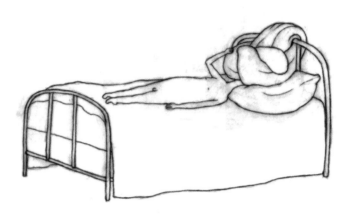

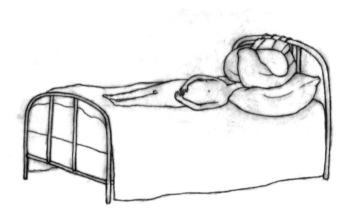

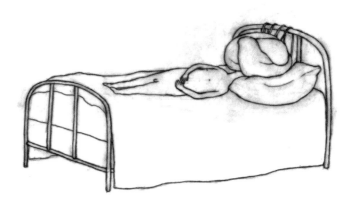

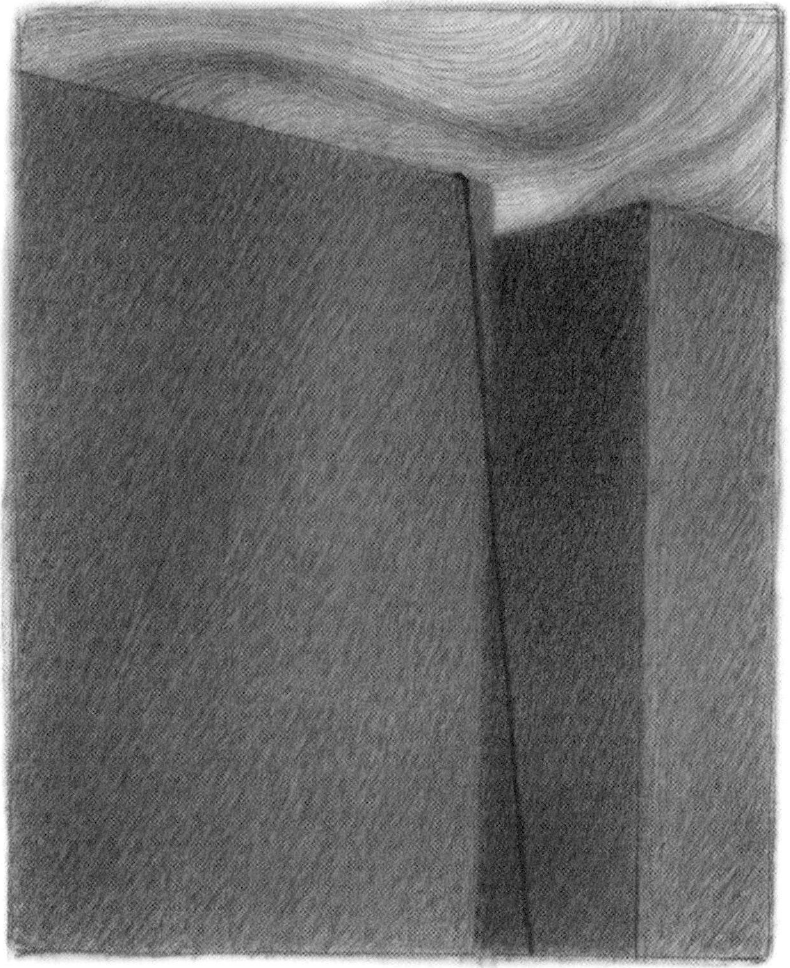

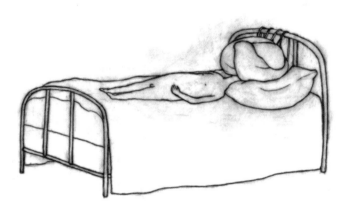

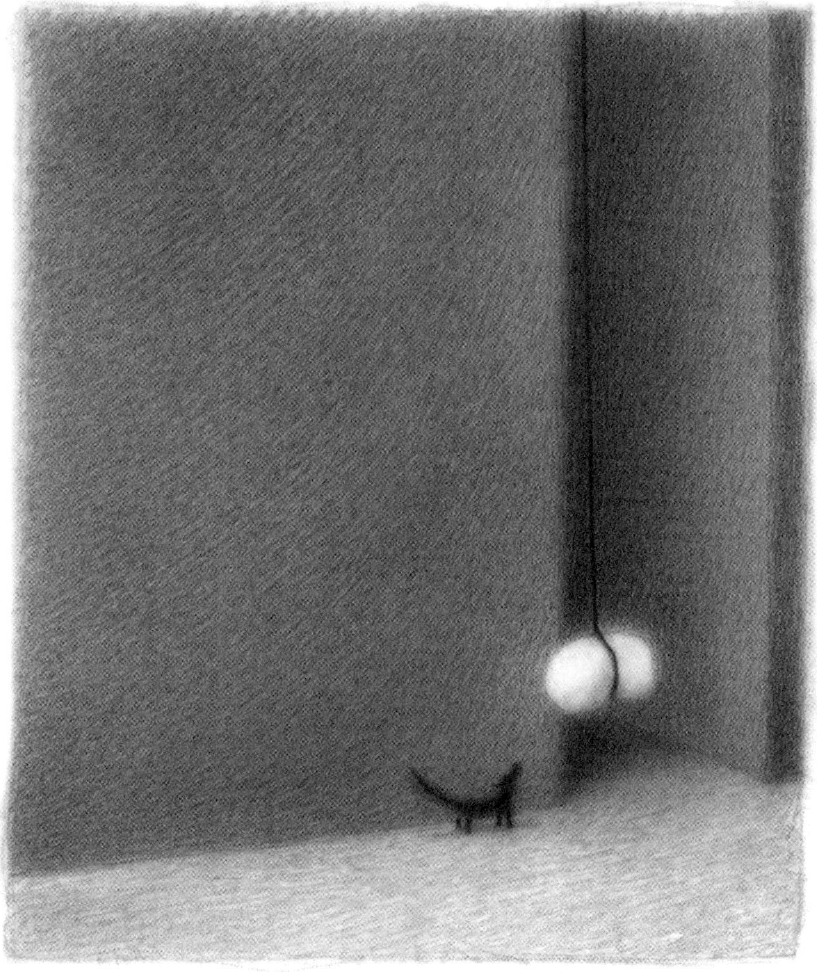

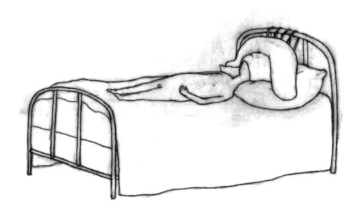

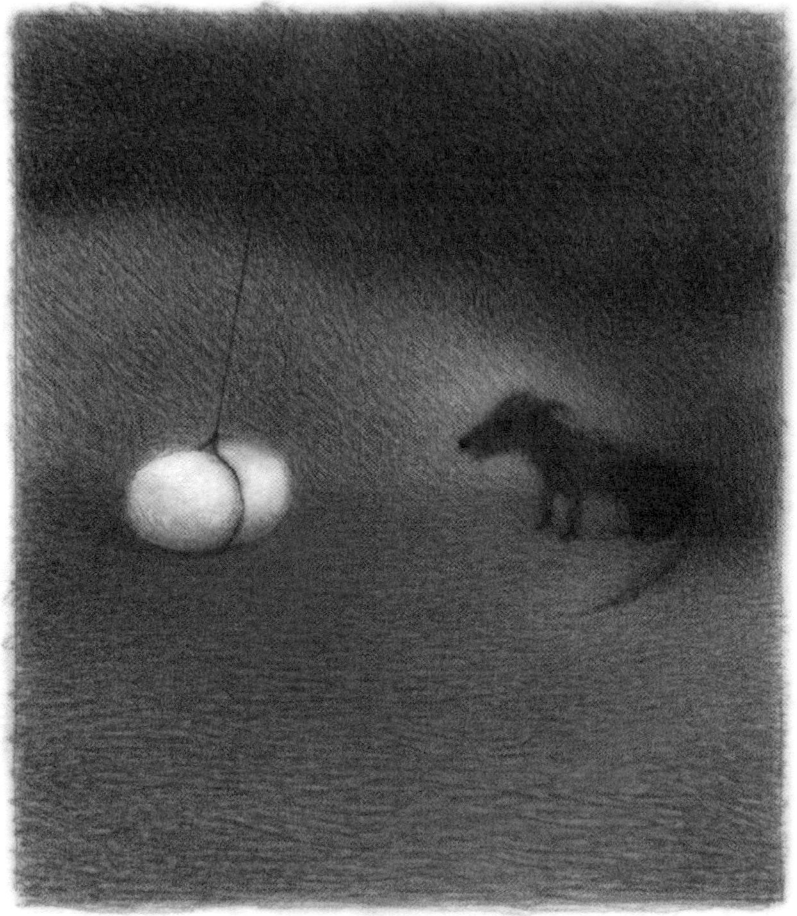

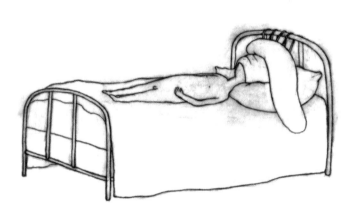

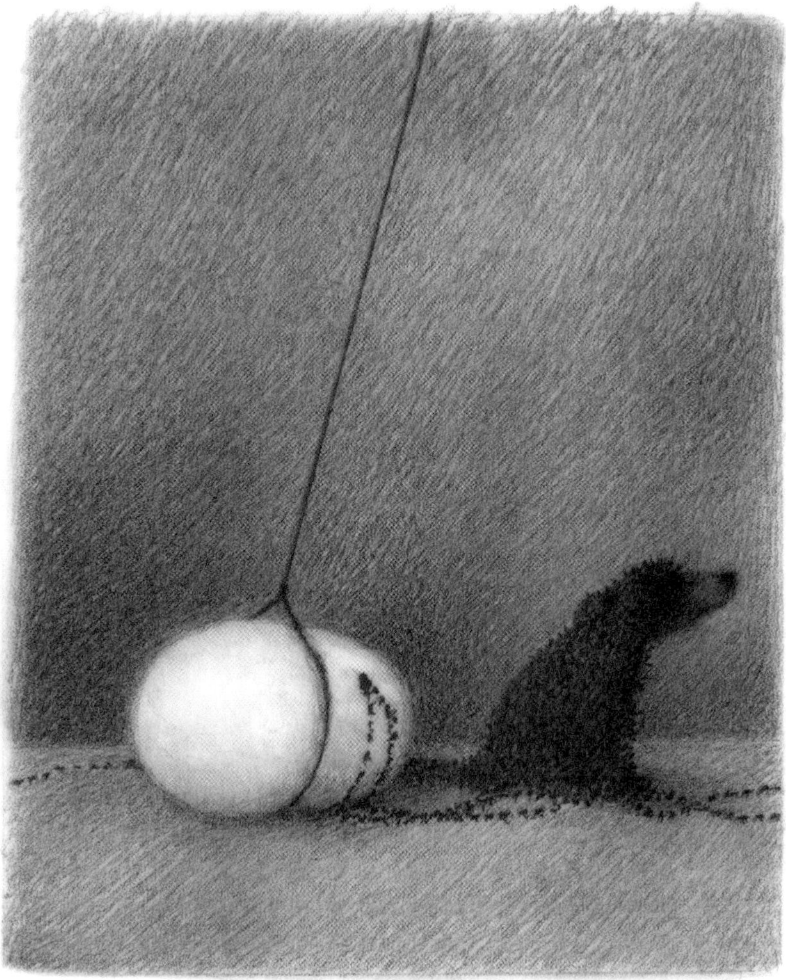

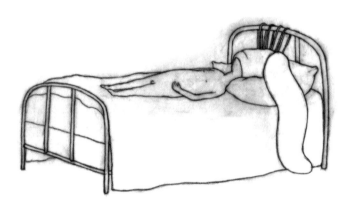

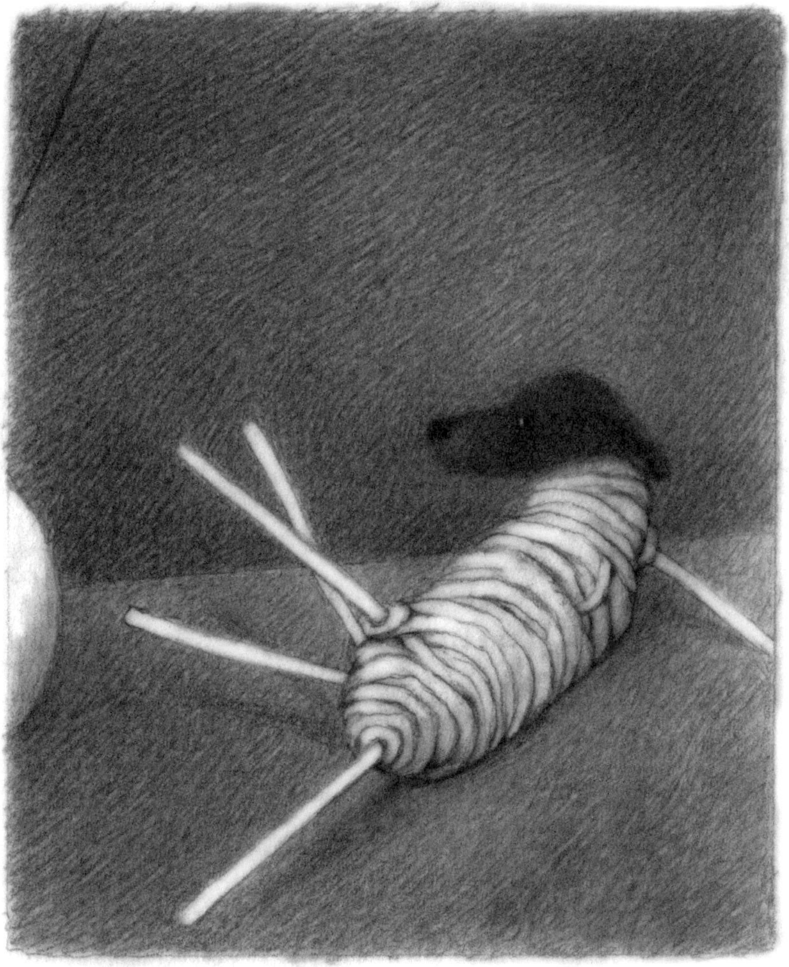

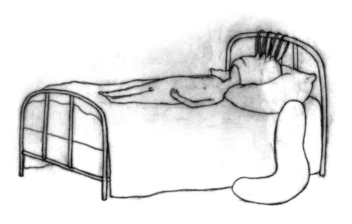

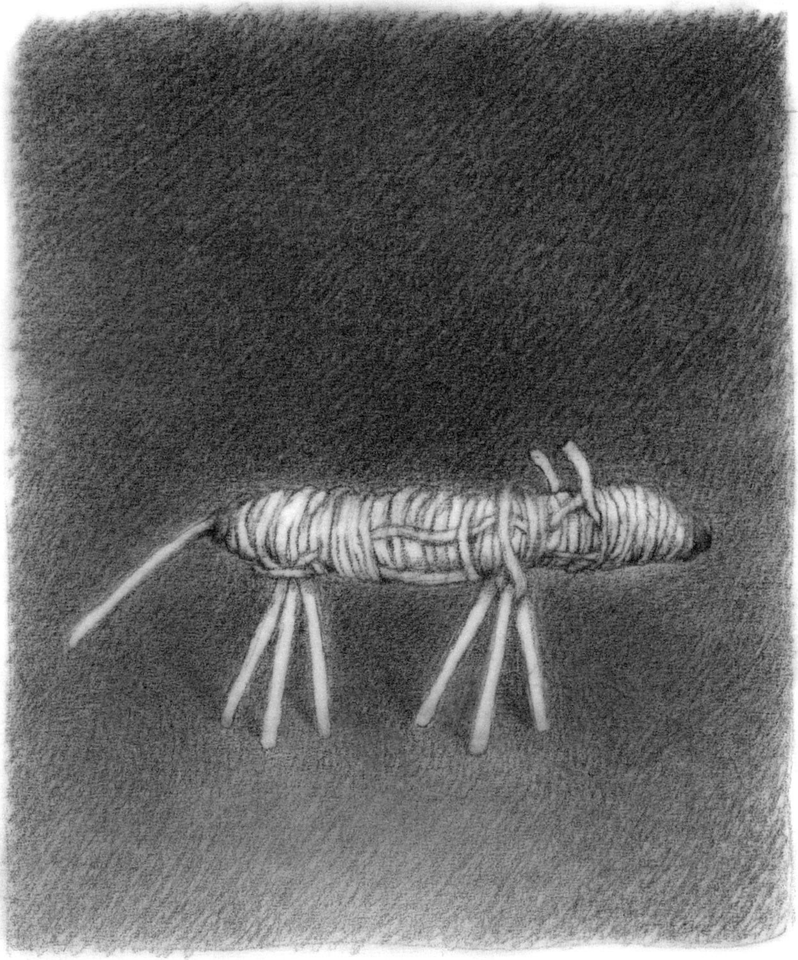

stage 4

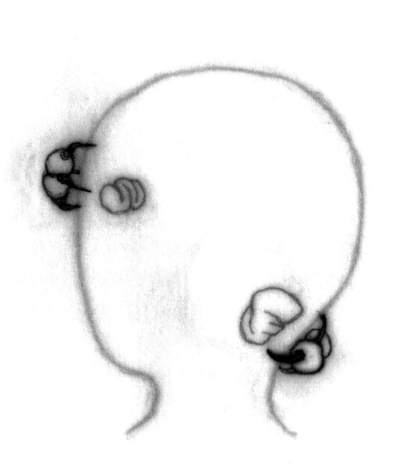

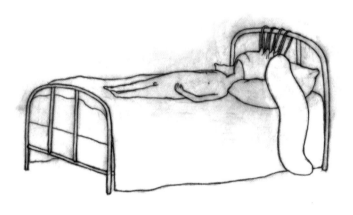

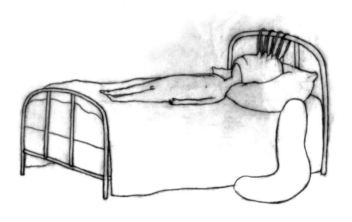

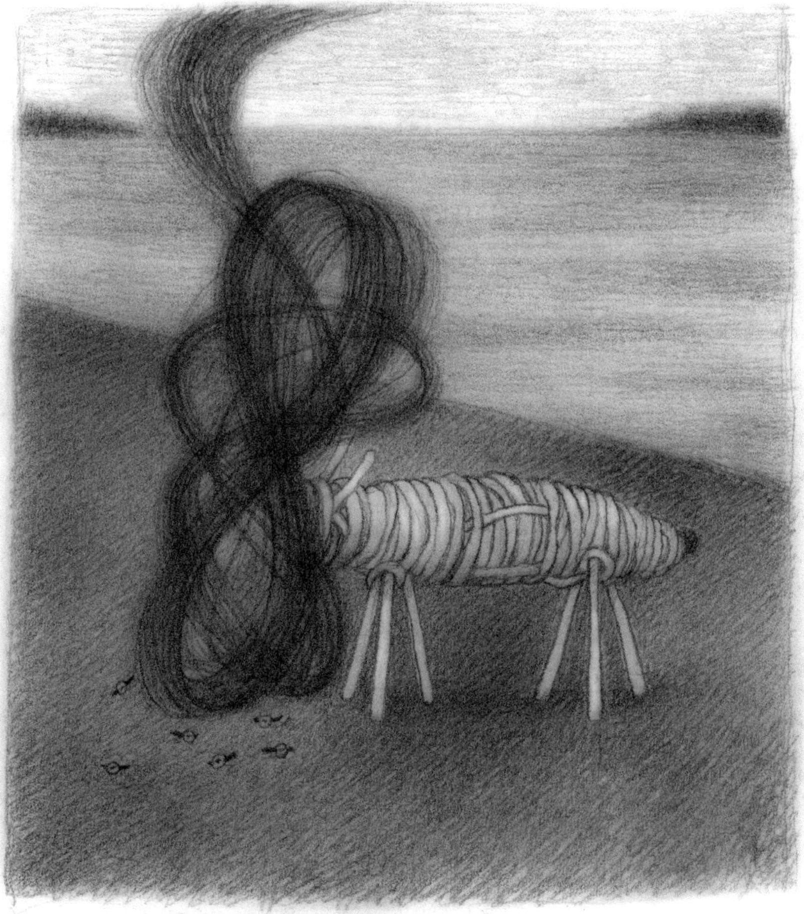

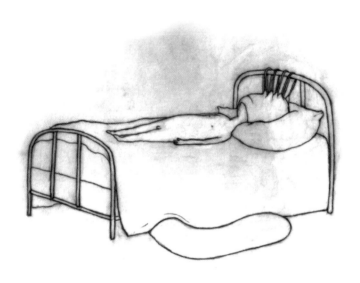

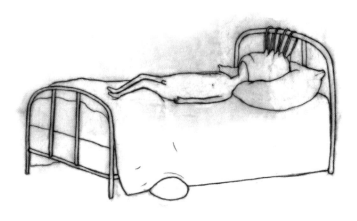

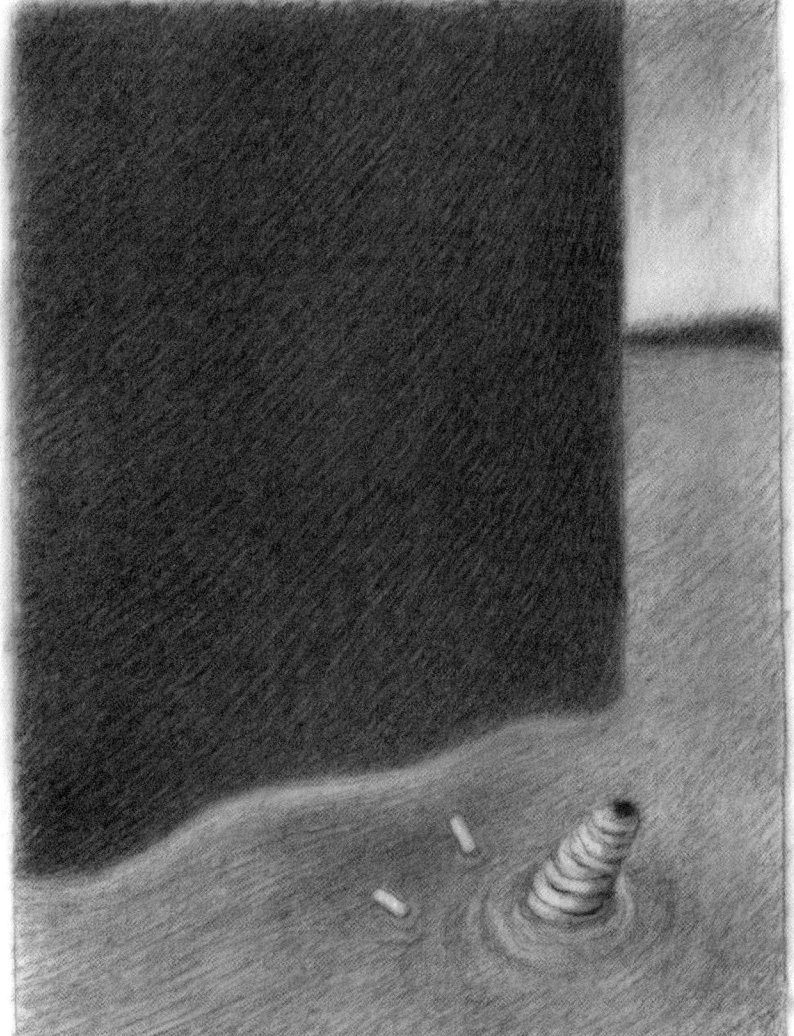

stage 5

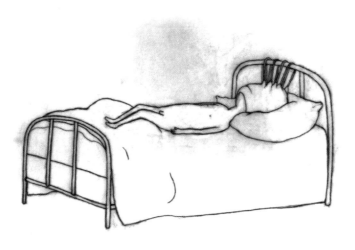

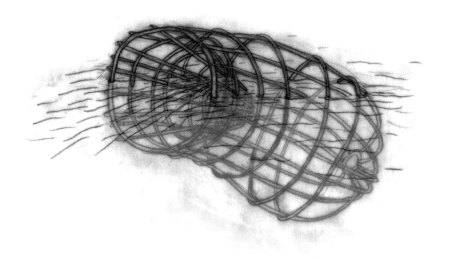

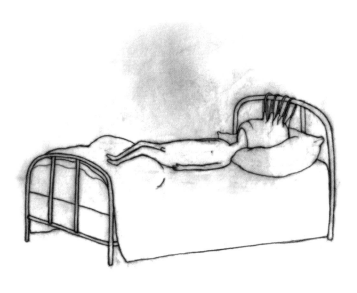

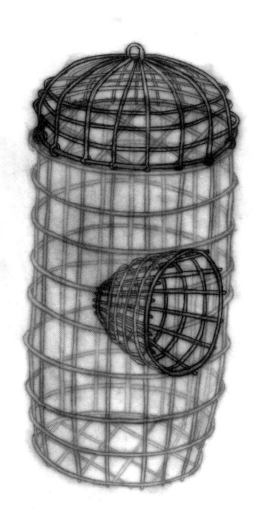

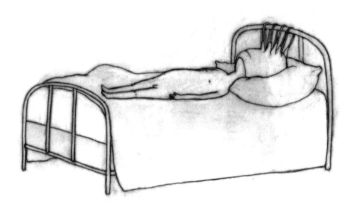

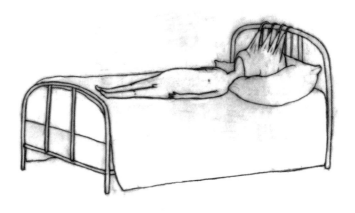

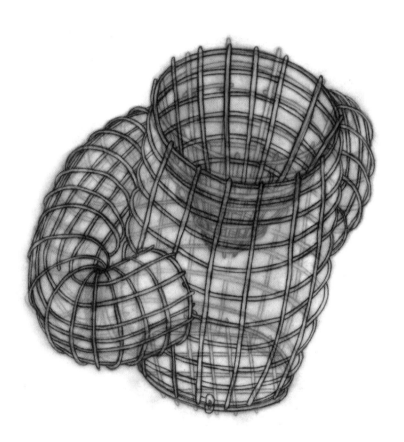

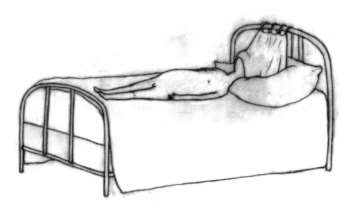

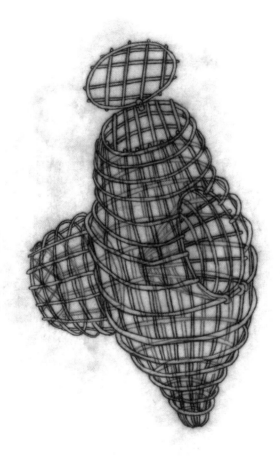

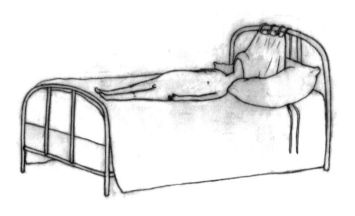

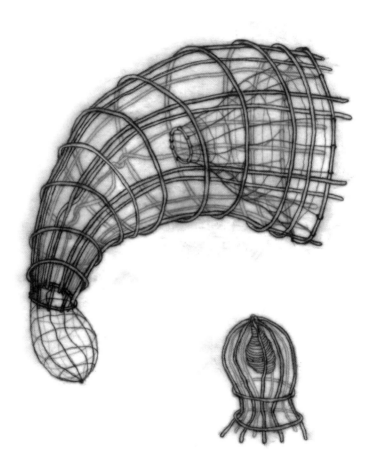

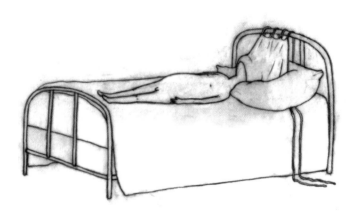

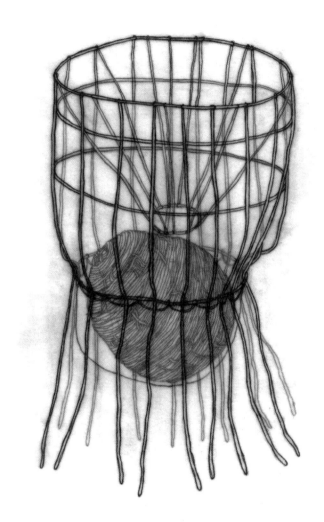

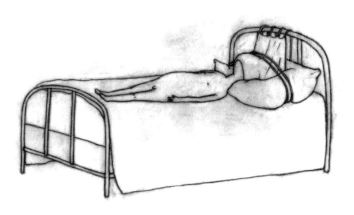

stage 6

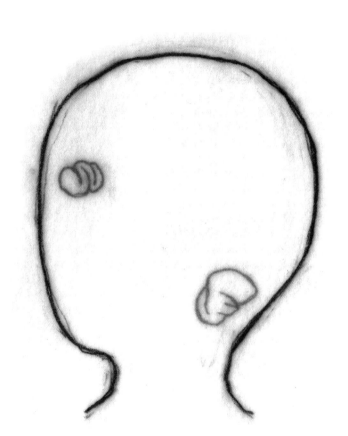

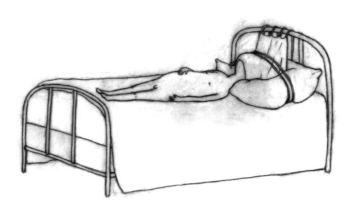

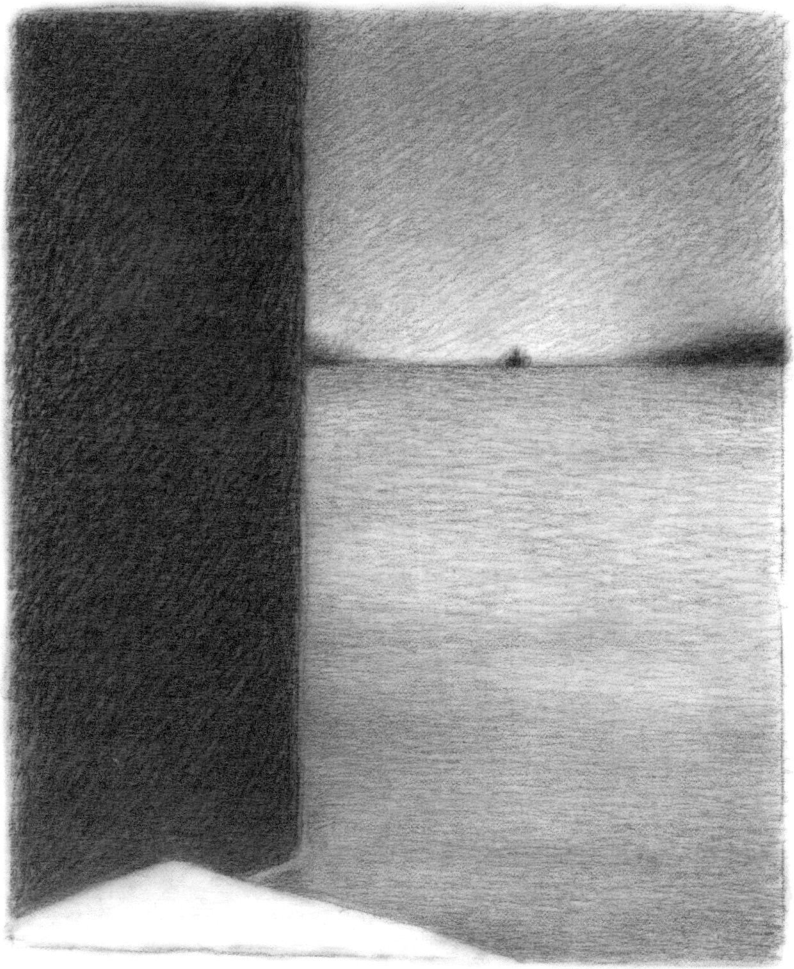

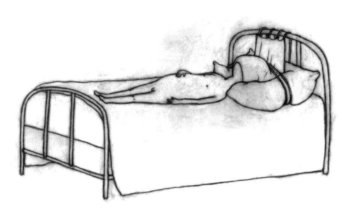

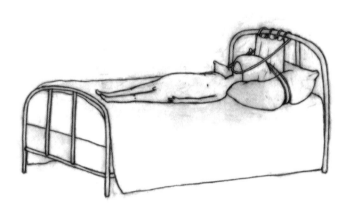

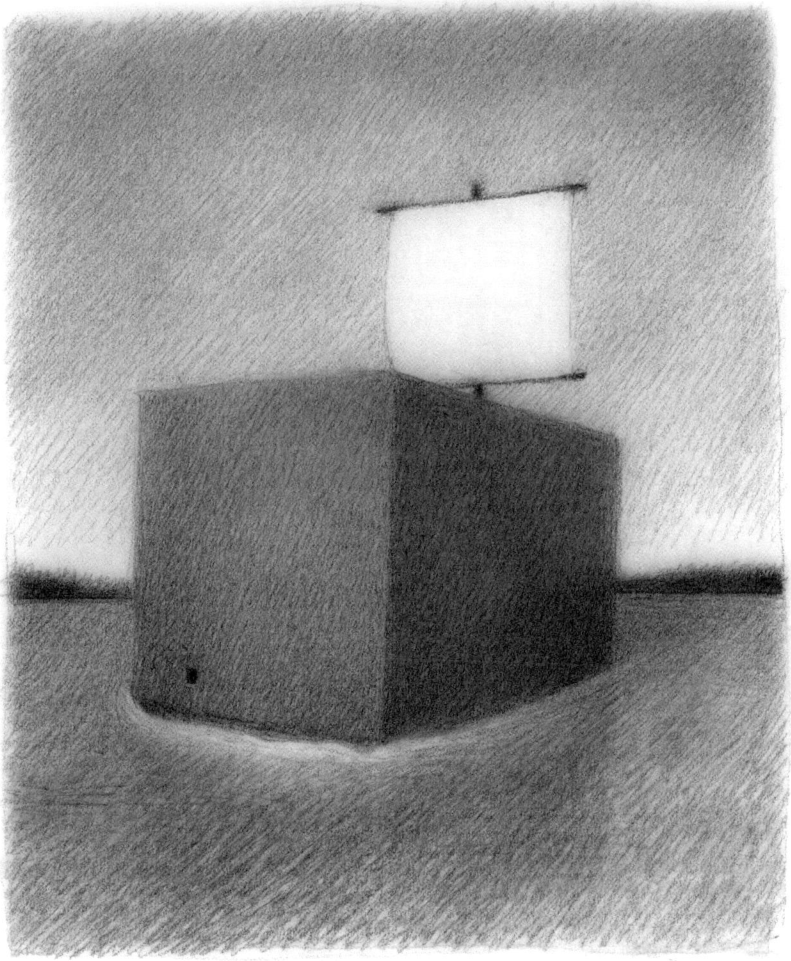

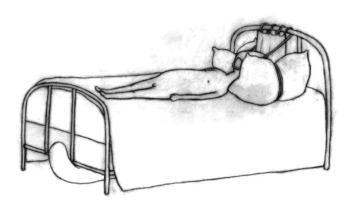

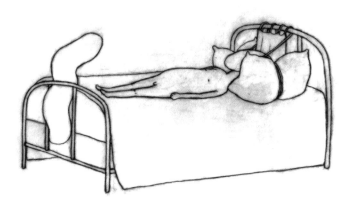

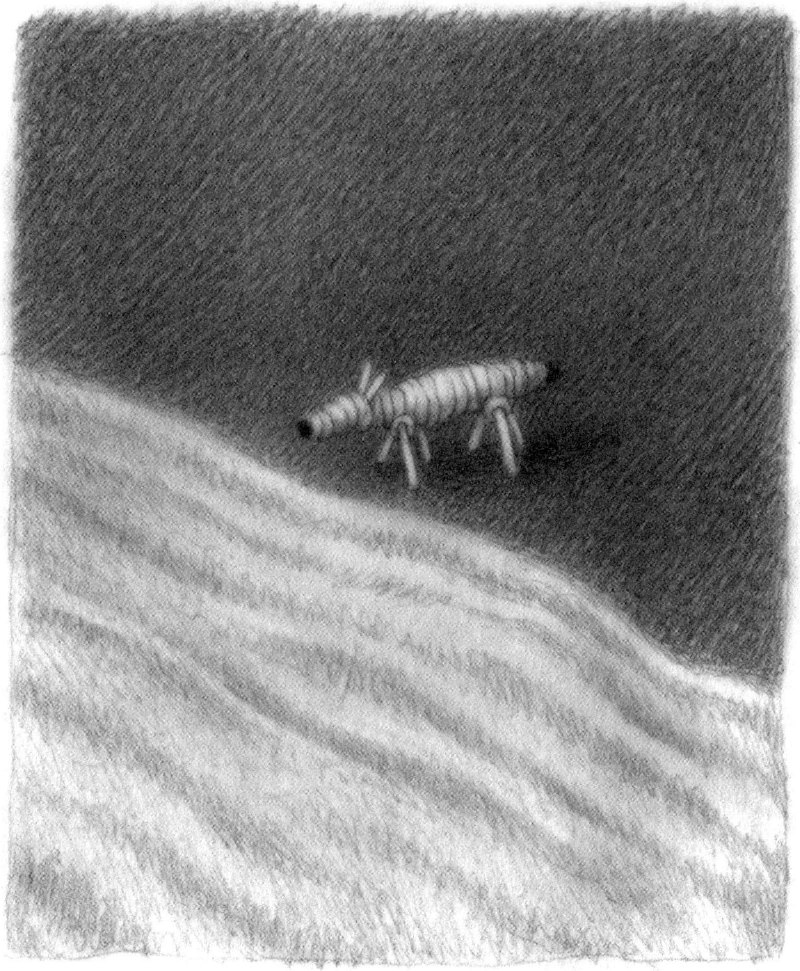

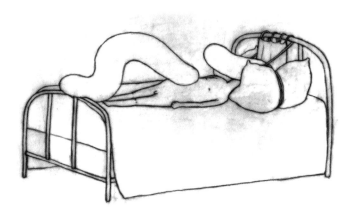

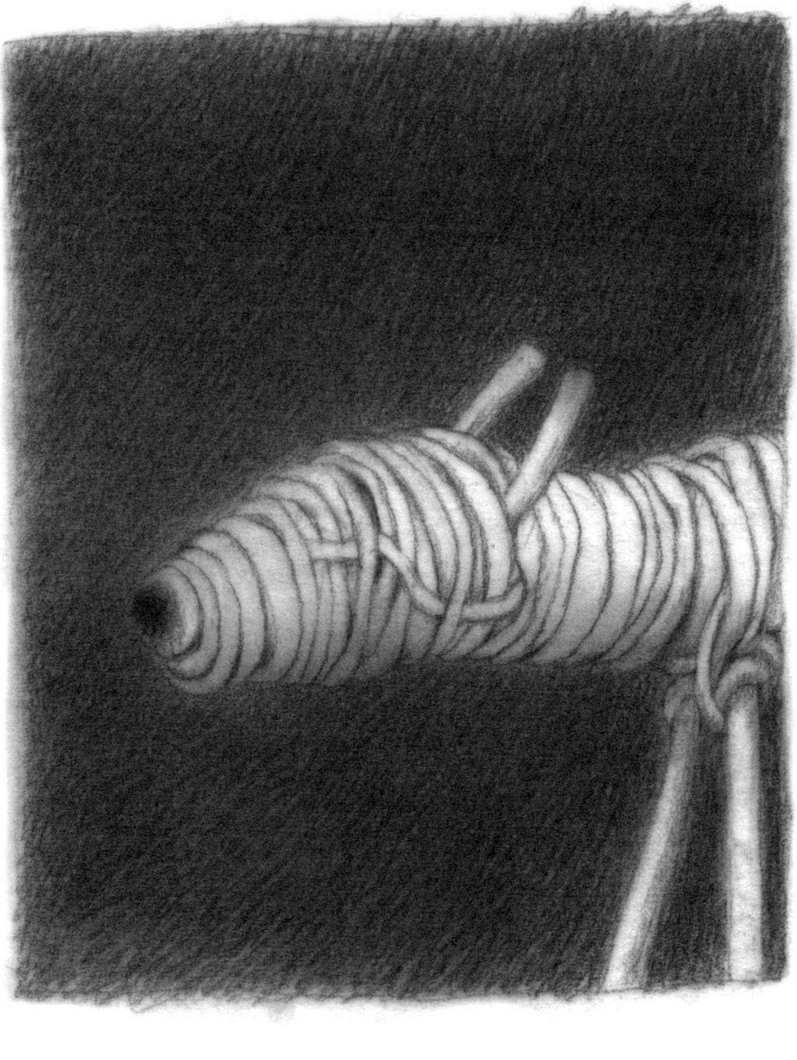

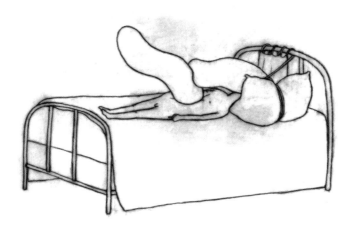

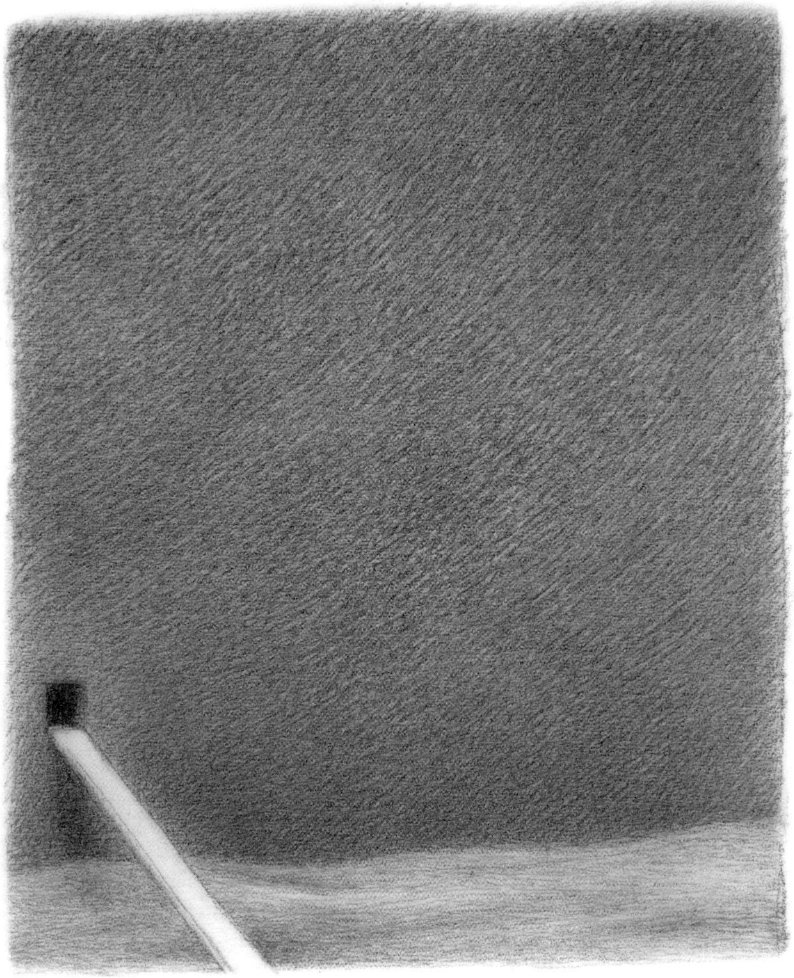

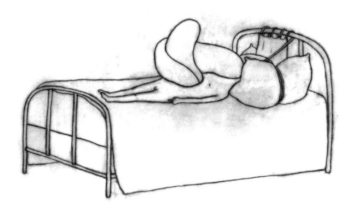

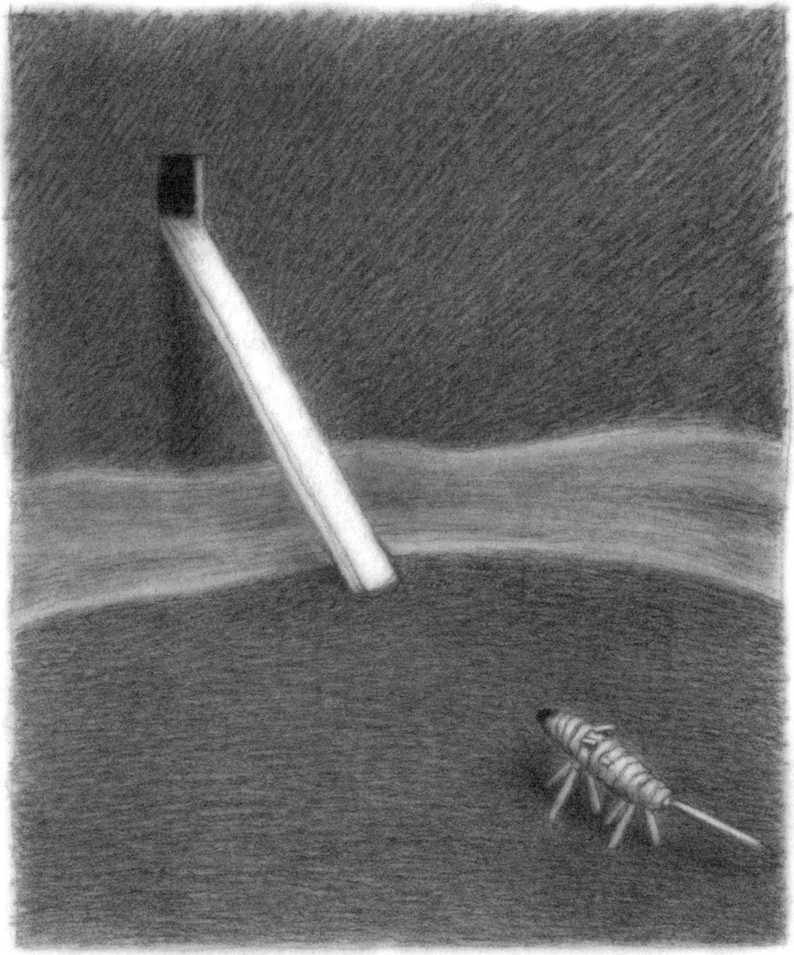

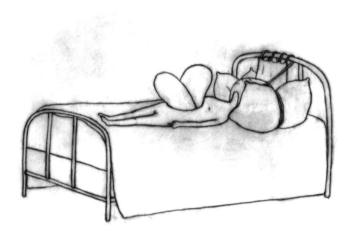

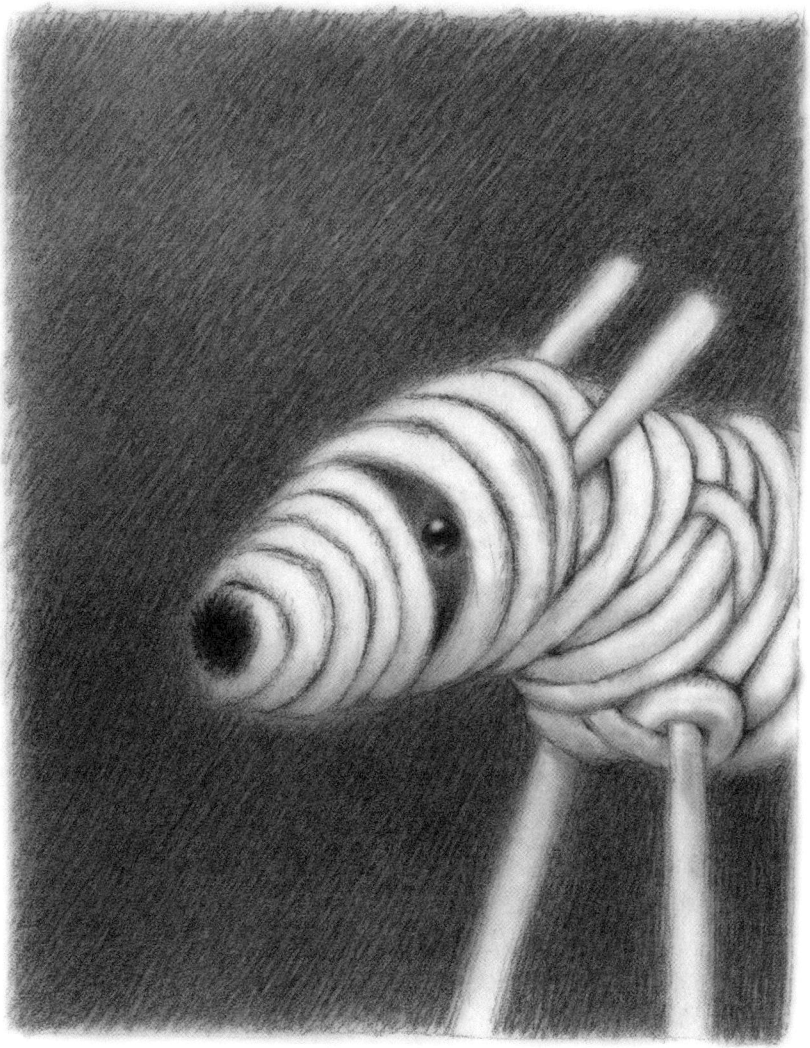

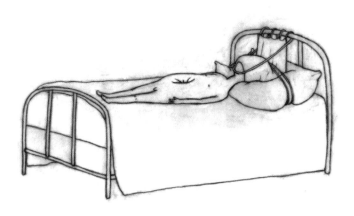

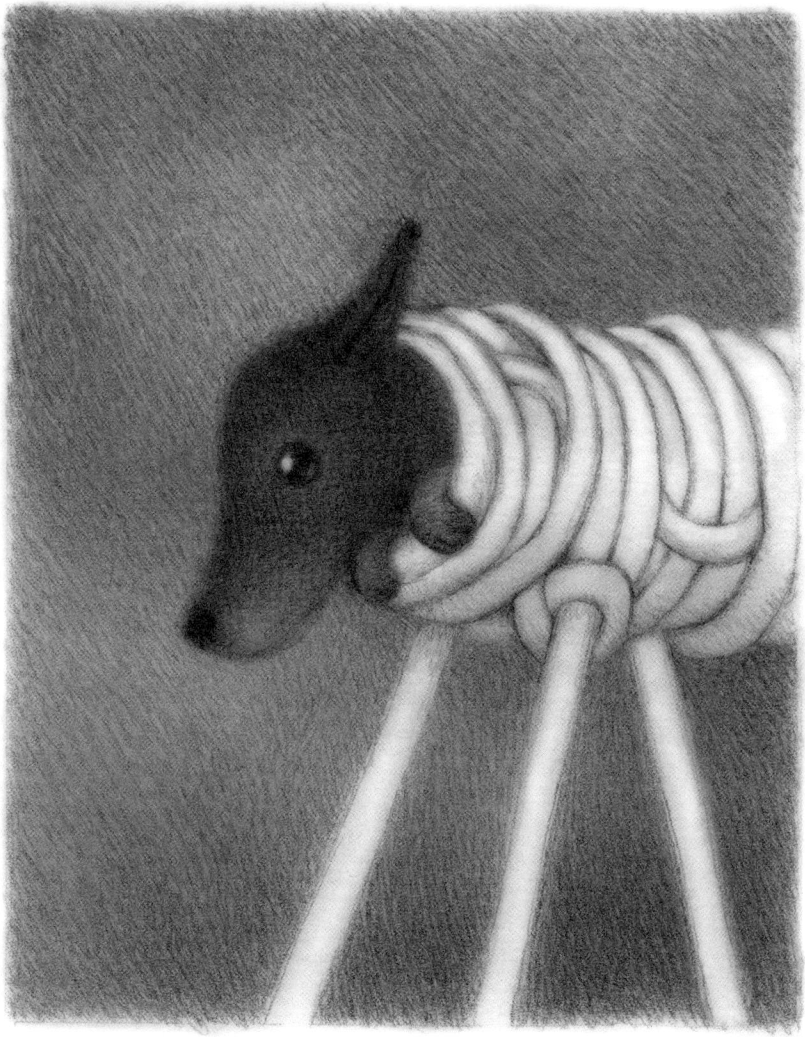

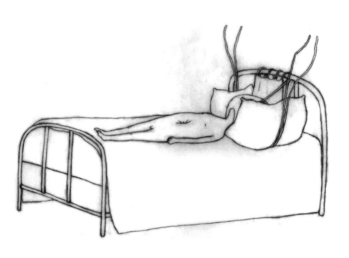

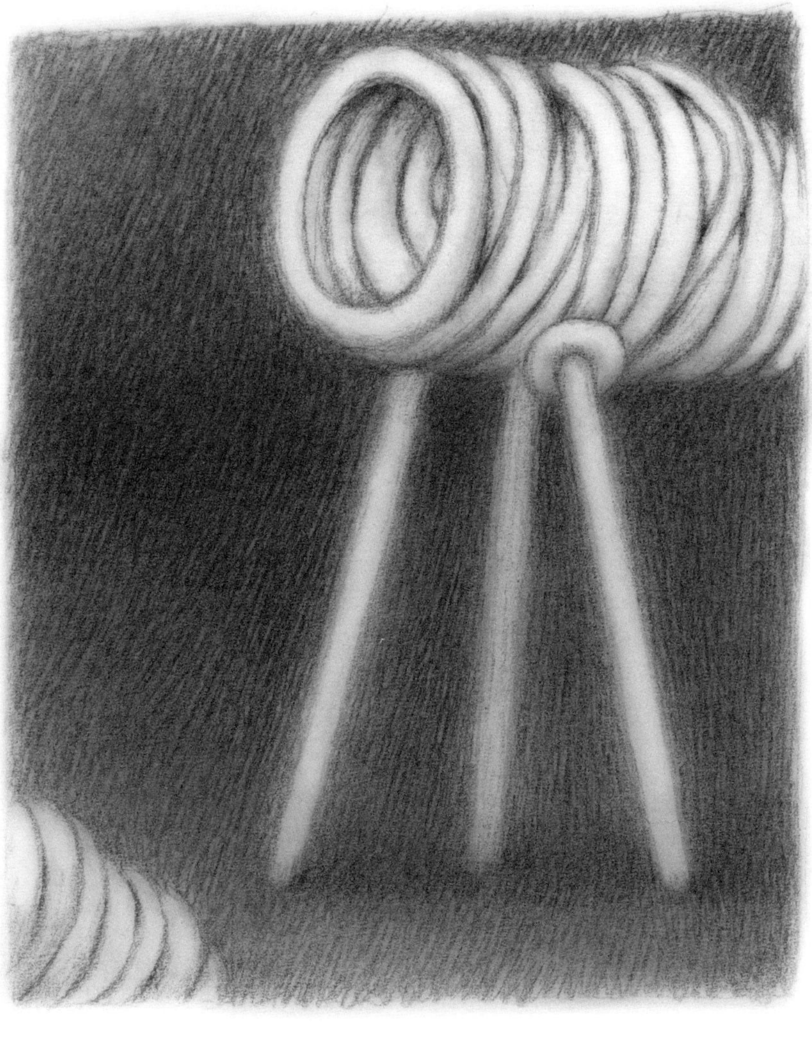

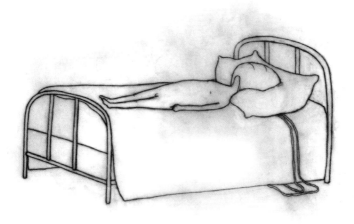

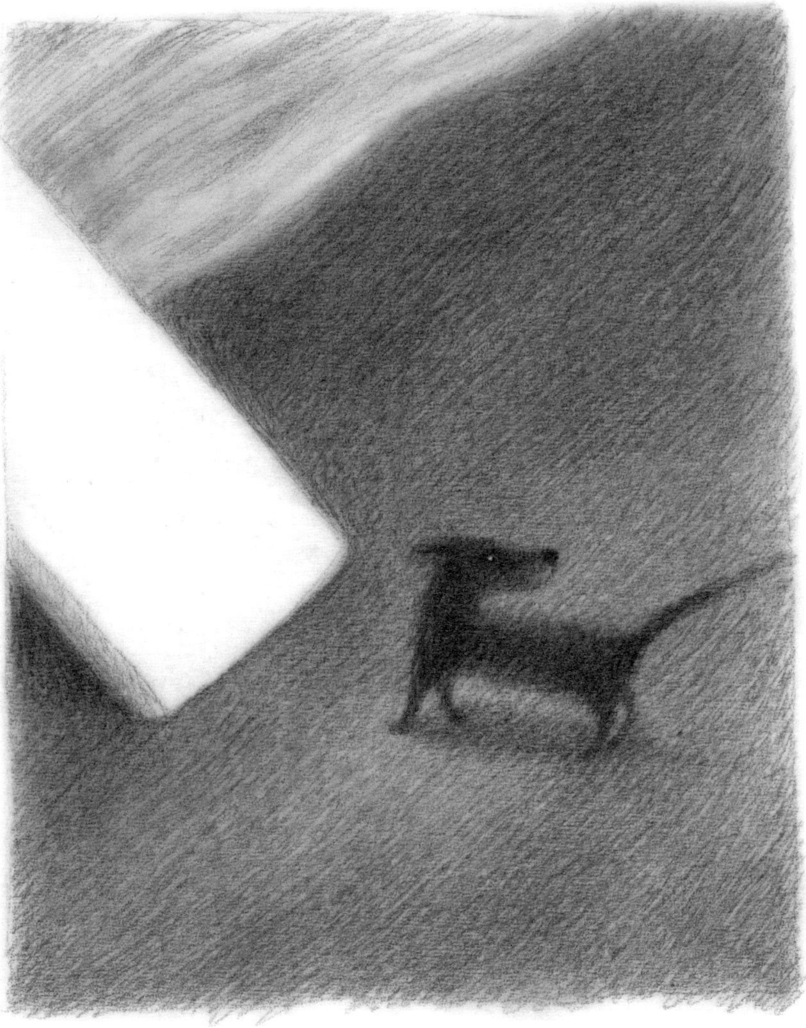

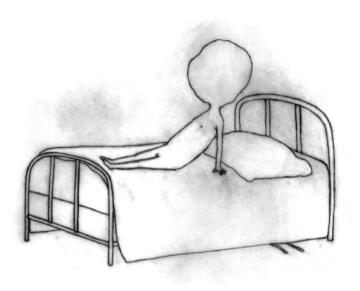

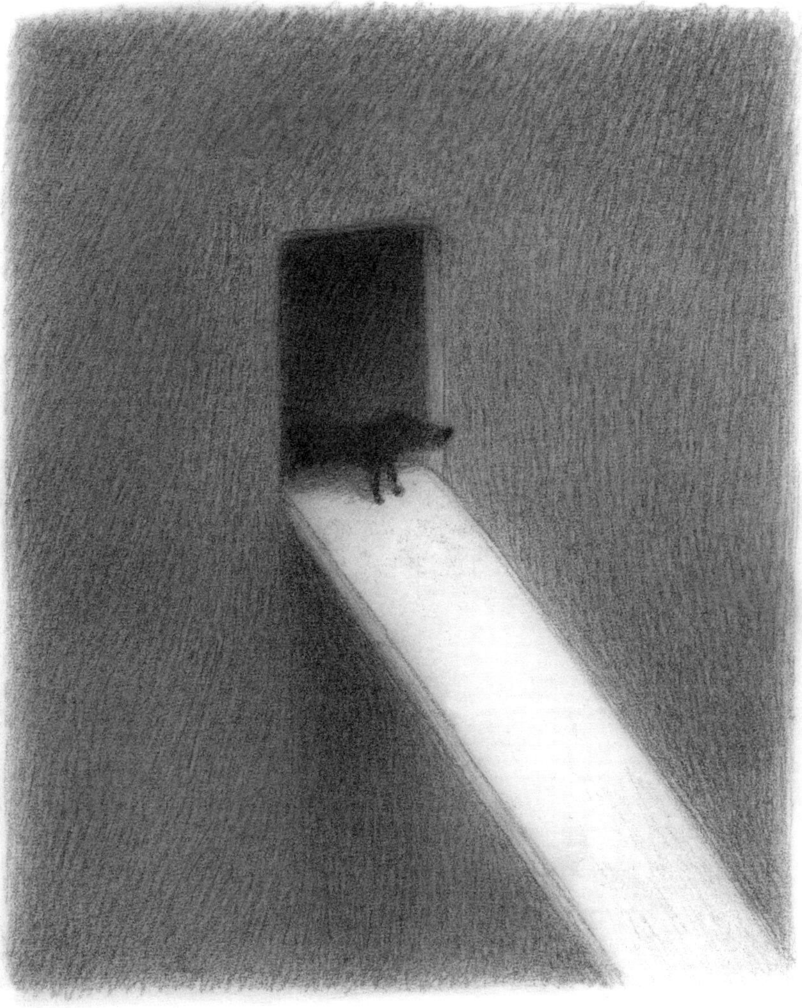

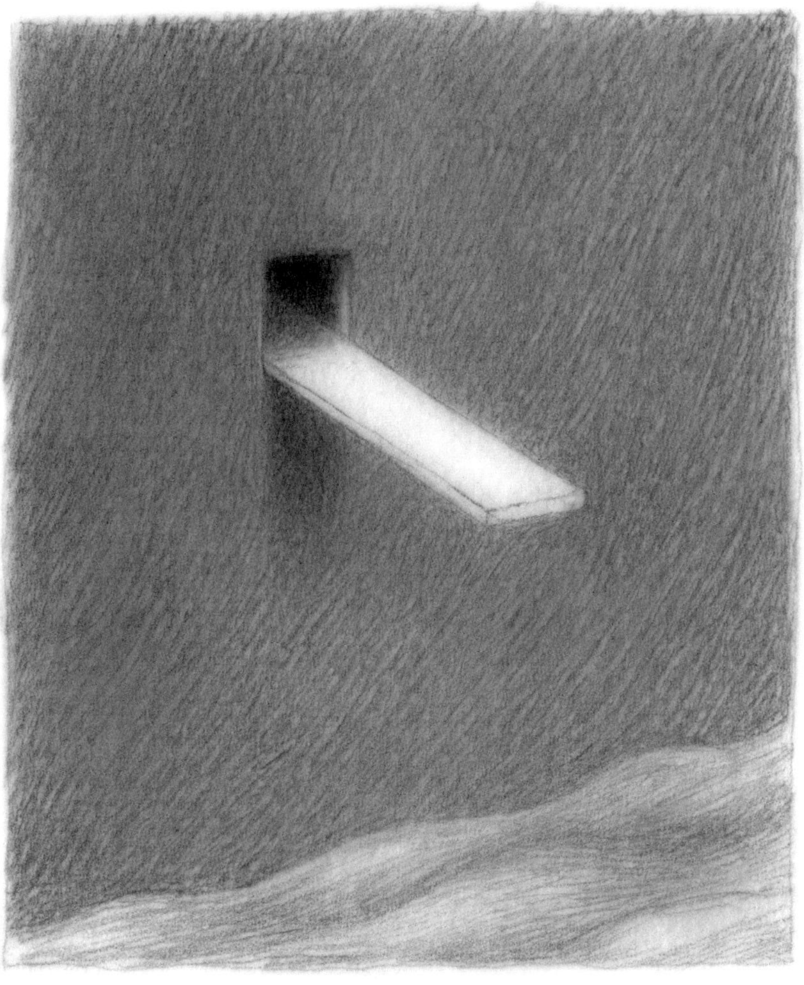

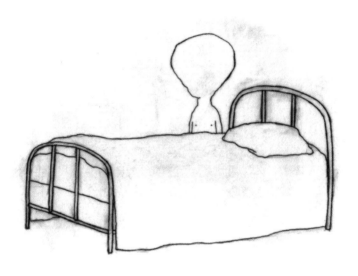

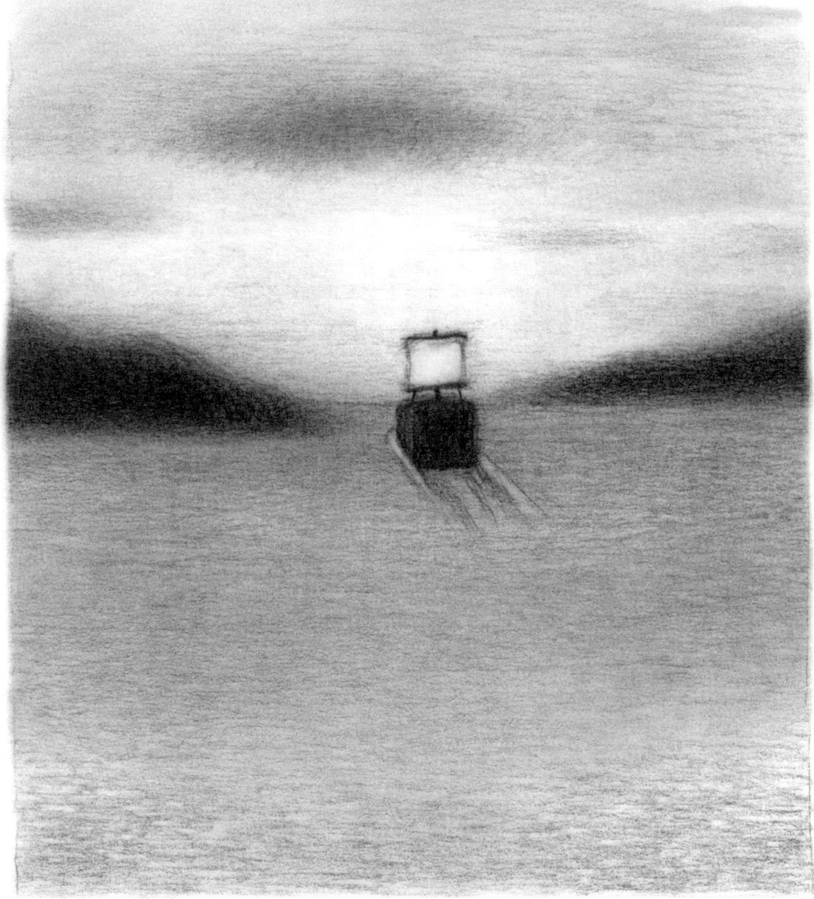

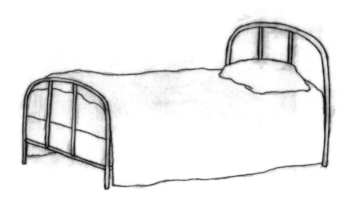

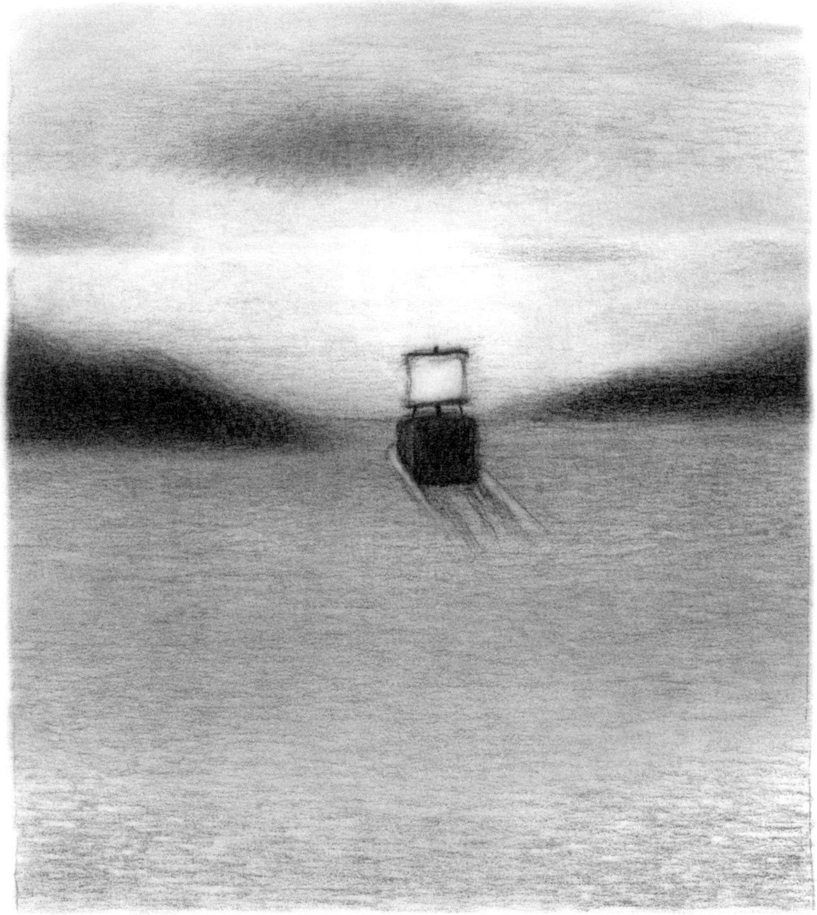

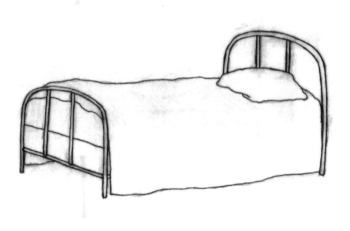